Rethinking IT

Outsourcing:

The New IT Offshoring

Frank Howard

Foreword by
Chiranjoy Das
CIO, SimpleTire

Larchmont Publishing

For permissions, contact:

Larchmont Publishing
3470 Olney-Laytonsville Road, #296
Olney, MD 20832 USA

www.LarchmontPublishing.com

Direct inquiries to: info@LarchmontPublishing.com

Printed by CreateSpace

First Printing, 2018

ISBN 978-0-9998732-0-5 (paperback edition)
ISBN 978-0-9998732-1-2 (Kindle edition)

Copyright Registration Number: TXu2-084-528

Library of Congress Cataloging-in-Publication Data:
Howard, Frank D.
         Rethinking IT Outsourcing: The New IT Offshoring / Frank D. Howard.
Library of Congress Control Number: 2018907120

Printed in the United States of America

Dedication

This book is dedicated to my wonderful wife and life partner, Denise. Your unwavering support, encouragement, and patience amaze and sustain me.

Acknowledgements

Writing and publishing a book is no small undertaking, and I am fortunate to have worked with so many talented professionals who made it enjoyable and rewarding. I am deeply indebted to you all and extend my heartfelt gratitude.

Many thanks to Richard Burke, Keith Crispin, and Jon Rance, my colleagues at AoteA Global Services. You gave me the inspiration to write this book, and your contributions made it possible.

Anna Paige, Content Pro & Consultant (www.APaigeWriter.com). It may be a cliché in the Acknowledgements section of many books, but in this case, it's true: This book would not have been possible without you! You possess an understanding of both strategy and tactics, business acumen, and a sense of humor, too. That's a rare combination and you were invaluable to me as I wrote this book.

Who Should Read This Book

Can you relate to any of the following statements?

- The idea of IT outsourcing is new to me and I'd like to learn more.
- I'd like to try outsourcing some IT work, but I've heard some horror stories, so I'm not sure it's worth the risk.
- I tried outsourcing IT work to a provider in India (or elsewhere) and it was a disaster. If I knew of a better way to mitigate the risks, I'd try again.

If any of those thoughts has ever crossed your mind, this book is for you! The good news is that traditional outsourcing is on its way out, along with its associated headaches. So, if you have mixed feelings about outsourcing because of all the negative things you might have heard or experienced personally, we hope you can put those aside and open your mind to a new paradigm: It's called IT offshoring.

We wrote this book with a surprisingly broad range of readers in mind:

- Leaders in business, government, academia, and non-profit organisations--in other words, anyone who is responsible for achieving bottom-line results and organisational objectives
- IT professionals such as C-suite executives and managers who oversee software development and other critical areas within organisations
- Human resources professionals who would like to learn a novel way to increase retention of star performers and other key employees in their IT departments
- Forward-thinking entrepreneurs seeking innovative ways to gain a competitive advantage by bringing value to their market
- Anyone interested in global talent mobility, and the role offshoring plays in it, in our increasingly connected world
- Anyone with a jaundiced view of outsourcing who is open-minded enough to learn how offshoring is superior to outmoded outsourcing models

Table of Contents

Foreword

Being in the IT industry for almost 27 years, I have encountered many challenges associated with running businesses around the globe. Rendition of those challenges, however, is not necessary because Frank does an exceptional job of elaborating them, especially when it comes to outsourcing. I have been involved in the outsourcing business since the early nineties, and Frank's account in this book is déjà vu all over again, as this brings back memories of experiences over the last decades with various outsourcing companies, small and big.

Frank has been in the middle of the growth and proliferation of IT outsourcing in the U.S. for more than a few moons. With this experience under his belt, he gives a clear perspective of the pitfalls and advantages of sending jobs to one country as opposed to another. Each country presents different sets of advantages and problems, many of which may not be transparent to the eyes of an untrained IT executive. Frank's international experience on the ever-shifting arena of IT outsourcing has been bundled concisely in this book, especially the potential of East-Africa and the upside of outsourcing to East African countries.

Certain perils of outsourcing are overlooked by most companies in the rush to meet the bottom line, but it almost always comes back to haunt them. One should go through all the criteria that Frank has laid out in this book before deciding to outsource. These criteria should be carefully evaluated because loss of productivity, morale and, above all, the reputation of the company—not to mention security hazards—can be imminent if the correct process is not followed. Frank has provided a checklist in this book that delineates the exercise that any company needs to go through in order to make a prudent decision about IT outsourcing.

I have worked with IT outsourcing companies in no less than 15 countries and, in doing so, I have learned many lessons the hard way. I wish I has this book when I started my IT career. Whether it is an international regulation or a simple hidden cultural issue, such factors, small or big, can ruin a business's critical projects and time to market, not to mention costing hundreds of thousands of dollars. Even the most rigorous due diligence can potentially skip some of the obvious issues which can come back to bite the decision of a CIO and expose a company to threats defiling a company. It's a quagmire I have seen many companies fall into, endangering its best products, services and customer satisfaction.

I felt compelled to write this foreword, not only because of the mistakes I have made in my career, but also to help other CIOs make the right decision. This book should be a must-have guide for every top IT executive in the country and deserves a place on the desk of every IT professional. Beside IT executives, all other business folks must read this book as well because outsourcing has permeated other areas, such as medical coding, as well as other industries which may have little to do with IT. Some examples are customer support, operations and sales of insurance and travel companies.

I am glad to see Frank taking a comprehensive, yet "wizard-like," approach to this subject, whereby the reader is steered through the decision-making process of IT outsourcing step by step. I applaud his effort in educating us all, and I am confident that all readers will benefit from it. It is a casual read, whether you are in the airport or getting ready to present IT an outsourcing proposal to the Board of Directors. I wish Frank and AoteA Global Services success in guiding every IT top executive.

Happy IT Outsourcing!

Chiranjoy Das
CIO, SimpleTire
Recipient of CIO100, Analytics50 & DigitalEdge50 awards
Advisor to Gartner's AADI (Application Architecture, Development & Integration)

A Special Message from the Author

Dear Reader,

I am an American living in the United States and publishing this book in the United States. Yet, it is written in British English or "the Queen's English," as some say. This is unusual, although my colleagues at AoteA Global Services and I made this decision to reflect the global nature of our operations; our founder and CEO lives in New Zealand, our operations are based in East Africa, and we have sales offices in several countries around the globe. Paperback and electronic copies of the book will ostensibly be read in many different countries.

So, if you are accustomed to reading British English, I trust you won't mind that the author is American, and the book was published in the United States. And, if you're accustomed to reading American English, I trust you won't mind reading British English. The differences are minor and don't interfere with comprehension of the material presented.

Now, if you want to talk about major differences, something that really matters, start a debate regarding who drives on the wrong side of the road...

Frank Howard

Introduction: What is IT Offshoring?

Thinking about outsourcing some technical work to a third party? Don't bother doing it the old-fashioned way. There's a new business model that lets you gain all the benefits while avoiding the pitfalls associated with traditional IT outsourcing. It's called IT *offshoring*. This book tells you about an easy way to get started.

IT offshoring takes the gamble out of conventional outsourcing. Now, you can sidestep the usual problems—like hidden costs, security vulnerabilities, time zone challenges, and contract negotiation hassles. Perhaps best of all, you can mitigate the risks. In fact, we believe you can put 90% or more of the risk of outsourcing behind you, just by practicing the new IT offshoring model.

If you're a newbie to outsourcing, IT offshoring will give you a leg up, because now you can dodge the dangers that go along with outsourcing the old way. If you've already tried outsourcing IT work and got burned, you can relax. IT offshoring means your old outsourcing troubles are over!

Sound intriguing? This book explains how IT offshoring works and tells you the numerous reasons why it is superior to the old school outsourcing model, and far less risky, too. Although cost savings is the usually primary driver for sending IT work overseas, you'll see that IT offshoring offers many other benefits as well. It eliminates the downsides of traditional outsourcing and lets you enjoy advantages like these:

- Reduce your operating costs
- Improve your company's focus
- Gain access to world-class capabilities and talent
- Offload functions that are time-consuming or hard to manage
- Gain access to resources that aren't available internally
- Retain your best and brightest employees
- Reduce recruitment and hiring costs

This book also tells you what steps you'll need to take if you want to open your own offshoring facility. Don't have the budget for that? Don't worry! You can still have your own overseas branch office. We have an effective, low-cost solution for you. In this book, you'll learn how you can leverage the time and talent of your offshore resources and begin reaping the rewards of IT offshoring right away.

Ready to learn more? Read on!

Chapter 1   How Outsourcing Transformed the IT Industry

The idea of outsourcing started in the 1980's when companies outsourced to external suppliers those functions for which they had no internal resources or competency—for example, printing and fulfilment services. As the 1990's approached, organisations began to shift their focus toward cost-saving measures. Eastman Kodak's decision to outsource their IT systems in 1989 created a revolution, prompting other corporations to rethink their business strategies, too. By the early 1990's, high-tech giants, like Microsoft®, having recognised the huge potential outsourcing offered, led the way by adopting the new strategy. Before long, the entire IT industry was using outside suppliers for certain types of services.

The Early Days

One of the first in-house functions IT organisations tried to outsource was the Help Desk, which takes inbound calls from customers and tries to resolve problems. The Help Desk was a logical choice for this trial for several reasons. For one, a Help Desk is relatively self-contained and easy to manage. Moreover, because customers tend to ask routine questions, Help Desk workers can efficiently handle customer inquiries about off-the-shelf products, like Microsoft Office, with only minimal training.

Using a third-party outsourcing provider made it much easier—not to mention cheaper—to support customers across the globe. The advantages of outsourcing one's Help Desk were many. Calls from customers that came in during non-peak hours no longer went to voice mail to be answered the next day. If you outsourced work to several different time zones, your customers could get 24-hour support.

IT giants like Microsoft led the initiative for outsourcing the Help Desk function, and other organisations followed. Soon, companies began to realise just how much they had been overspending by keeping their support services in-house. With labour typically being one of a Help Desk's greatest costs, companies discovered that using *onshore*, *near-shore*, or *offshore* outsourcing services resulted in a significant reduction in labour costs, taxes, or both.

Wondering what the terms "onshore," "near-shore," and "offshore" mean? We'll go into more depth later, but here's all you need to know for now. "Onshore" refers to a company's home country, which is typically located in the Western World. So, with onshore outsourcing, a company uses the services of another company located its own country. "Near-shore" refers to a nearby country, which is often on the same continent. Near-shoring means using the services of a company located in another country that's close to yours. And, finally, "offshore" refers to another country that's located in a different part of the world. Offshoring involves exporting work from your onshore location to your offshore location. Usually, the parent company is onshore, and its offshore office is in a developing country that has a rich talent pool and offers significant cost savings, particularly when it comes to labour and infrastructure costs.

As the outsourcing trend gained momentum, companies gradually began shifting their Help Desk services to call centres equipped to handle a high volume of calls. At the same time, the Help Desk function began to evolve and adapt. The more sophisticated, proactive, and efficient the Help Desk became, the greater impact it had on the company's bottom line.

By the early 1990's, the overwhelming success of Help Desk outsourcing prompted companies to try outsourcing other core business functions, like back office operations, data processing, and human resources. These undertakings proved to be equally rewarding. Before long, what had originally started out as an experiment became a practice that took the IT industry by storm.

By the mid-1990's, outsourcing had become a customary practice in the IT industry. Companies were happily reaping its advantages but had not yet harnessed its full potential. The industry was on the cusp of a radical change that would be fuelled by a confluence of three unexpected events that was just over the horizon.

The Y2K Crisis Created an Overwhelming Need for Programmers

By the late 1990's, it had become alarmingly apparent that millions of computers were affected by an error that became known as "Y2K bug." The problem had originated in the 1950's and 60's when systems programmers decided to code dates using a six-digit format (that is, dd/mm/yy or, in the U.S., *mm/dd/yy*) instead of an eight-digit format (that is, dd/mm/yyyy or *mm/dd/yyyy*). The decision to shorten the year to two digits seemed practical in an era when computers ran much slower and resources like memory were much scarcer than they are today. At the time, the next millennium seemed so far away that no one considered these systems might still be in use 40 or 50 years later.

The discovery of the Y2K bug evolved into a crisis that generated global hysteria. Doomsday predictions sent the whole world into a panic. Media outlets hyped the millennium madness, referring to the situation as a "ticking time bomb." TIME Magazine suggested the possibility of an apocalypse on its January 18, 1999 cover, which read *"The End of the World!?!"*[1] Rampant reports spread the fear that critical systems would shut down one second after the stroke of midnight on December 31, 1999, bringing the world as we knew it to an abrupt end.

Companies scrambled to fix this programming nightmare. The prospect of diverting a crisis seemed impossible when a typical business computer system contained millions of lines of code written in multiple computer languages. How was it possible to sift through that much code and make all the necessary changes in time? There simply weren't enough programmers in the world for such a monumental task. The problem seemed insurmountable—not to mention, cost prohibitive. In the United States alone, the Federal government estimated Y2K-compliance upgrades would run about USD 100 billion. Some independent computer consultancy groups, like the Gartner Group, considered this estimate too conservative and put the costs closer to USD 1 trillion.[2]

---

[1] TIME Magazine. http://content.time.com/time/covers/0,16641,19990118,00.html (accessed December 22, 2017)
[2] Lehman, Dewayne. "Senate: Y2K Fixes Worth the Billions Spent." Computerworld, March 6, 2000. https://books.google.com/books?id=J2pCrhV7T2cC&pg=PA8&lpg=PA8 &dq=gartner+group+y2k+estimate&source=bl&ots=_a636eCkv_&sig=l NBccJ48Bkg6ascczbEaFWR_HM4&hl=en&sa=X&ved=0ahUKEwiNj5- AnpjUAhVhwVQKHYC0CHwQ6AEISTAJ#v=onepage&q=gartner%20gro up%20y2k%20estimate&f=false. (accessed October 15, 2017)

Governments and countries across the globe worked together to address the Y2K crisis and many liberalised their worker immigration policies. In the U.S., Federal agencies instituted stopgap measures by establishing new guest worker visa categories that allowed great numbers of foreign IT workers and created other policies that made outsourcing the most obvious solution to the Y2K problem.

And so, Y2K came first in the series of climactic events that helped set the stage for the explosive growth of outsourcing.

India Flooded the Market with Cheap Skilled Labour

When the Y2K frenzy created an unprecedented need for programmers, Satyam Computer Services Ltd. of Hyderabad, India stepped up to offer a solution.[3] Satyam was an early pioneer in the arena and had already developed some successful Y2K debugging methods. This positioned Satyam—and the city of Hyderabad—as a top Y2K operation centre.

Hyderabad's officials wasted no time before beginning to court American technology giants like Microsoft. Tech firms were mutually attracted because English is widely spoken in India, and the country's strong education system emphasises subjects like science, technology, engineering, and mathematics (STEM).

Before long, computer training schools cropped up throughout Hyderabad offering three-month training certifications. The graduates of these programs were promoted as "experts" and IT companies snapped them up as quickly as Hyderabad could churn them out. By 1998, at least 10,000 of

---

[3] Goldenberg, Suzanne. "Boom time in India as the millennium bug bites." The Guardian, December 29, 1998. https://www.theguardian.com/world/1998/dec/30/millennium.uk. (accessed October 15, 2017)

these graduates were leaving for the U.S. each year. Hyderabad's tech boom spread to other Indian cities and, before long, India became known as the world's top IT outsourcing provider.

The sudden and plentiful availability of cheap labour was the second advancement in the triad of events that contributed to the explosive growth of outsourcing.

A Blue-Chip Lawsuit Changed How the IT Industry Hires Workers

A third development—this one, unrelated to the Y2K crisis—also played a pivotal role in transforming the IT industry. It began in 1992 when a group of Microsoft employees filed a high-profile class action suit against the tech giant. The group claimed that, to avoid the costs associated with carrying full-time employees, Microsoft had chosen to keep them on as temporary workers over the long term instead of offering them permanent jobs. The lawsuit charged that Microsoft had cheated these workers out of millions of dollars in benefits and stock purchase options.

The legal battle raged on for 8 years, until 2000, when Microsoft settled and agreed to pay USD 97 million in damages to as many as 12,000 current and former workers who had been employed between 1987 and 2000.[4] The case generated a great deal of publicity and had a deep impact on the entire the IT industry. Thereafter, Microsoft instituted a new policy that limited temporary jobs to a term of one year and required workers to take a break before assuming their next assignment.

---

[4] Greenhouse, Steven. "Technology; Temp Workers at Microsoft Win Lawsuit." New York Times, December 13, 2000. http://www.nytimes.com/2000/12/13/business/technology-temp-workers-at-microsoft-win-lawsuit.html. (accessed October 15, 2017)

But this new policy did not benefit Microsoft nearly as much as its previous "permatemp" arrangement had. So, the company found a more profitable solution. By looking to offshore staffing services to meet their needs for temporary workers, Microsoft capitalised on the rapidly growing pool of cheap foreign labour. It didn't take long for the industry to catch on and, soon, other IT companies began following Microsoft's lead.

Now There's an Even Better Way to Outsource

Many factors played a part in making outsourcing a standard IT industry practice. However, the Y2K crisis, the sudden and plentiful availability of cheap labour, and the class action lawsuit that exposed Microsoft's use of a shady hiring practice were among the most significant drivers for outsourcing early on.

The industry's shift toward outsourcing has helped many firms enjoy lower costs and increased profits. Outsourced labour is cheaper because employers do not pay the benefits and other carrying costs associated with permanent, full-time employees. This offers significant savings when you consider that the combined costs of insurance, vacation, and other benefits for an individual employee are typically equal to the employee's annual salary. Outsourcing also eliminates the costs of recruiting, hiring, and retaining employees.

Since the early days, outsourcing has grown and expanded exponentially, and companies have found even more innovative ways to make outsourcing work. In 2016 alone, the global market size of outsourced services was just short of USD 76.9 billion.[5] That same year, the revenue of the global IT

_____

[5] https://www.statista.com/statistics/189788/global-outsourcing-market-size/

business process outsourcing (BPO) industry was USD 24 billion.[6]

When you consider the benefits companies reap by outsourcing, it's hard to imagine a better solution. However, as you will see in Chapter 3, traditional outsourcing has some serious downsides. The good news is, there is a better mouse trap that overcomes the flaws in the traditional model.

So, move over, IT outsourcing, 'cause there's a new kid in town! Far superior to outmoded outsourcing archetypes, the newest strategy is called *IT offshoring*. And, that's what this book is about. You'll learn there's a lot to love about this exciting, new way of doing things. But before we dive into offshoring, let's talk a bit more about old-style outsourcing models, and why **they don't work**. The next few chapters lay the foundation for understanding the weaknesses inherent in traditional outsourcing models and explain the main reasons why the old way of doing things is no longer the best option in today's global market. Once you understand the limitations of old-style IT outsourcing, it will become patently obvious that IT offshoring is the best way to maximise flexibility, productivity, and creativity, and increase profits.

---

[6] https://www.statista.com/statistics/189800/global-outsourcing-industry-revenue-by-service-type/

Chapter 2   How IT Offshoring Works

IT outsourcing is a broad umbrella that encompasses several different staffing models. Before we talk about IT offshoring, it's important to understand how conventional outsourcing works so we have a basis for comparison. So, first, let's review the two most common earlier-generation outsourcing models:

- Contract workers
- Traditional overseas IT services firms like India's Tata, InfoSys, and Wipro

Hiring IT Contractors

The contractor model relies on temporary employees to augment full-time, permanent staff. Contractors are not considered part of an organisation's headcount. Once a popular practice, the contractor model was largely demolished in 2000 by the class action "permatemps" lawsuit that ended up costing Microsoft USD 97 million, as we discussed in Chapter 1. The flaw inherent in the original version of this model allowed companies to avoid employee carrying costs and deny benefits— such as health coverage, pensions, and stock options— to long-term workers by classifying them as temps.

Even though the Microsoft lawsuit sent a loud message, some organisations have chosen not to listen and are now finding themselves in hot water. In a more recent development, four contractors in the U.S. filed a lawsuit against the State of Massachusetts for full-time status.[7] One of the employees,

---

[7] Abel, David. "'I'm a second-class employee.' Contractors suing state over full-time status." The Boston Globe, November 23, 2017. http://www.bostonglobe.com/metro/2017/11/23/second-class-employee-contractors-suing-state-over-full-time-status/zTwtASrBKTDJZ5qfHsbsTL/story.html. (accessed November 25, 2017)

Michael McHugh, has been protecting wetlands for the state's Department of Environmental Protection for the past 27 years. McHugh is just one of thousands of long-term contractors who have never received health insurance benefits, vacation days, or a pension from the State. These contractors are asking the Court to reclassify them as regular, full-time employees and reimburse them — plus, up to 10,000 other current and former contractors — for years of lost benefits and compensation. If the group wins the case, it could cost the State of Massachusetts hundreds of millions of dollars. Clearly, it's just too risky to use contractors as a permanent substitute for full-time employees.

Some companies are using a newer version of this model that's more strictly regulated. The adaptation requires companies to hire workers who are employed by temp agencies that offer their employees paid vacation, health insurance, and other basic benefits.

With this type of arrangement, a firm can easily reduce the number of permanent, full-time workers it employs. When business is good, a company can staff up its organisation with temps, as needed. When business is bad, these workers can be let go. Because temps can be let go without affecting headcount, it often becomes easier for companies to avoid "real" layoffs. Thus, the company preserves public opinion and continues to appear robust and profitable, despite having instituted aggressive cost saving measures.

Although the temp agency arrangement offers some advantages over hiring permanent, full-time workers, the agencies still pass on some of the costs. And, they charge a commission. Typically, temp agencies will charge employers twice the employee's salary. However, because temps are not offered benefits like employee stock purchase plans and pensions, their carrying costs are lower than those for permanent, full-timers. But most importantly, there's no commitment, so employers can choose to cancel—or, just not renew—a temporary worker's contract.

Contracting foreign workers:

The contractor model also lends itself to contracting with foreign outsourcing consulting firms—like India's Tata, Infosys, Wipro, and others—for staff augmentation. These high-priced body-shoppers will also supply foreign workers to their customers' onshore facilities. In the U.S., with the advent of the H-1B guest worker visa, IT organisations began contracting with consulting firms to supply an agreed-upon number of workers to do certain IT jobs or run certain IT domains both at home and abroad.

A major problem associated with using these third-party consultancies is cost. The top ten outsourcing firms in India have formed a type of oligopoly, making it impossible for smaller players to compete. Their cost structure is quickly obliterating this type of contractor staff augmentation business because smaller companies can't afford it and big companies have the resources they need to create their own solutions. Nevertheless, this model continues to be highly profitable.

Hiring a Traditional Overseas IT Services Firm

With this onshore/offshore model, a small team of onshore workers is supplemented by a large team (sometimes as many as 90% of the total) of offshore resources.

As you'll see a bit later in this book, this model is considerably different from offshoring in many ways. One primary distinction is that, unlike true IT offshoring, the onshore/offshore model uses large consulting companies—typically, Indian firms like Tata, Infosys, and Wipro—to staff offshore IT organisations. These third-party firms employ foreign workers—again, typically Indians—who never become integrated with the company contracting their services.

13

Often, these workers are not formally tested or certified. And, frequently, their English language skills are so poor that the offshore team must communicate through an interpreter. Moreover, because the contracting company does not get the opportunity to vet the workers assigned to them, consulting firms frequently slip junior-level people into large teams as a way of training their own employees.

To add to the problem, sometimes one consulting company is swapped out for another to save money, or for some other reason. This always results in disruption and time lost while the workers at the new agency get up to speed.

With the onshore/offshore model, work is typically done during off hours because the onshore and offshore facilities are usually located a great distance apart, in vastly different time zones. This mandates the need for liaisons on each side who communicate information between them. Also, in many cases, offshore facilities are on different holiday schedules than their onshore counterparts. Operating on different schedules often has a negative impact, particularly when deadlines are tight.

As you will see, IT offshoring solves *all* these problems and more.

The New Model: IT Offshoring

More recently, a newer outsourcing scenario has emerged. Multinational corporations have increasingly begun opening their own offices overseas. This outsourcing model is called *IT offshoring* and, until recently, it was only an option for major players, like Microsoft, with big budgets and unlimited resources.

The facilities owned by major, multinational corporations were originally called "global captive centres" or "captives," for short. The newer name for them is "Global In-house Centers" (GIC's). In this book, we use the more familiar term "captive."

Captives are technology and (non-IT-related) business process offshoring (BPO) centres that are owned and managed by a parent company and used only for that organisation's internal activities. Whereas parent companies are typically located onshore, their captives tend to be in foreign countries, where the cost of doing business is low. *The workers at a captive centre are legal employees of the parent corporation and do not belong to an offshoring vendor.*

The motivation behind a captive is to save money by cutting out the middleman—meaning the third-party outsourcing firms and offshoring vendors. Owning your own captive centre is cheaper in many ways, with the low cost of foreign labour being its primary advantage. You still incur overhead, infrastructure, and other costs associated with building and owning facilities abroad, but it typically costs much less than running a similar facility onshore.

The Difficulties Inherent in Establishing Your Own Captive

Captive centres save money and drive down costs in the long run. However, the ramp-up costs are substantial, as is the investment in time. Establishing such a facility is a slow process that involves a significant amount of risk. It is time-consuming and expensive to scout out the perfect location, research all the applicable laws, and then build or procure a facility that will need to be furnished, outfitted with the proper technology, and staffed with workers who will need to be screened and hired.

Doing business in a foreign country typically involves mountains of red tape and a lot of time spent waiting for paperwork to be processed, because things often move much more slowly overseas, especially in developing countries.

Additionally, you need to be astutely aware of all the government legislation, regulations, and local ordinances relevant to global captives in the area where you have chosen to do business. Fees for obtaining permits can be expensive. Legal issues are a major concern—you might be out of compliance and not even know it! Operating in non-accordance to the law opens your company up to vulnerabilities, especially when it comes to the security of your data and intellectual property (more about that in Chapter 4). Some foreign governments keep tabs on global operatives by performing unannounced site visits or audits. And, penalties for violations can be steep.

Hiring resources to staff a captive centre is another expensive and time-consuming process that involves reams of paperwork. You need to consider costs such as work permits, passports, visas, lotteries, skills assessments, employee medical exams, plus all the legal fees and delays associated with those types of things. Vetting employees in developing countries can be difficult; you don't always know who you're hiring or whether you can trust them. When employing foreign workers, it's particularly important to stay current with the country's immigration laws. In many countries, companies are required to track changes in employee status and report that information to the authorities.

The above are just a few examples of the types of difficulties inherent in establishing and operating a global captive. It's easy to see how the initial outlay of cash makes this a cost-prohibitive option for all but the largest multinationals. Plus, there's the issue of all that time you spend waiting, waiting, waiting for the wheels to turn in a foreign country where processes can drag out due to bogged-down bureaucracies, and cultural and language barriers. Meanwhile, the work's not getting done and schedules are slipping. It all affects the bottom line.

You Don't Need to Own a Captive Centre to Do IT Offshoring

Although having your own captive centre might be an ideal solution, most companies can't afford the expense of building and operating one. But that doesn't have to stop you from offshoring some IT work. As an alternative, you can contract with an IT offshoring provider, like us at AoteA.

Offshoring providers own physical office space offshore and can help you set up your own overseas branch office. Such facilities are generally called "Offshore Delivery Centers" (ODC's). Because AoteA specialises in IT development services, we use the term "Offshore Development Center."

In addition to office space, offshoring providers supply overseas job candidates, so you can meet your staffing needs. Although the staff you hire work for you, they are managed by your vendor's human resources function, so you don't need to be involved overseeing day-to-day personnel issues. The offshoring provider also supplies the necessary equipment, as well as the appropriate security measures for data, internet, and access to the physical office space.

The Advantages of Offshoring with AoteA

For most companies wanting to offshore IT work, it makes a lot of sense to use an offshoring vendor. When you choose AoteA as your IT offshoring provider, you can enjoy all the advantages of having your own captive centre without any of the hassles.

Indeed, AoteA offers a hybrid solution that allows you to send IT work overseas without the problems, high costs, and wildly fluctuating monthly charges associated with traditional IT outsourcing firms. It's the next best thing to owning your own captive—in many cases, even better! Small and medium-sized companies can't afford the investment of time and money to go into a country suitable for offshoring. And some of the larger corporations don't have the time or inclination to create a captive centre for themselves. As you'll see later in this book, AoteA's unique business model makes us a *true* offshoring company, which is radically different than any old-school outsourcing firm.

You get your own turnkey branch office in East Africa that's set up and ready to go. (You'll see why East Africa is an ideal location a bit later in this chapter.) The building is already there, and we've already vetted and certified our workers. The appropriate safeguards are in place, so you won't have to worry about the security of your data or intellectual property. Nor will you need to keep track of foreign government regulations.

At AoteA, we've already done the legwork for you. And, we've come up with a solution that even small companies can afford. All you need to do is staff your offshore office by selecting the skills and resources you need from among the thousands of highly qualified workers in our talent pool. All of them are proficient in written and conversational English, with accents as close as possible to Western speakers. And, all are certified because they have passed our stringent technical skills assessment tests.

When you choose AoteA as your IT offshoring provider, you get to enjoy advantages like these:

- A dramatic reduction in costs
- No degradation in security
- A stable, flexible, effective branch office
- No time zone or language barriers between your onshore and offshore offices
- Quick ramp-up time
- The ability to ramp down when necessary without the pain and expense of layoffs in the home office

IT offshoring with AoteA offers you something even greater, too. When you work with us, you develop a personal relationship with someone who understands and cares about your company's goals and objectives. Together, we share a strategic vision and plan. You get to know and communicate with each member of your highly qualified offshore team personally, instead of relying on an interpreter, which often creates bottlenecks. And, you can offload your human resources function to us and trust us to manage your employees and deal with any staffing issues or personnel problems. All things considered, AoteA becomes a valued business partner to you in ways no traditional outsourcing firm can match.

You've already seen the many ways in which IT offshoring can save you money. Now, finally, with AoteA, you can cut the middleman out of the picture and eliminate the added expense of those overpriced, third-party outsourcing contractors. We don't send out bloated invoices every month like they do. In addition to saving on IT costs, offshoring gives you more control, too.

Later in this book, we explain our offshoring model in greater detail and show you how AoteA puts you back in the driver's seat.

Why East Africa?

We decided to open AoteA's first state-of-the art IT offshoring facility in East Africa, and now we are actively scouting out other East African locations where we plan to open even more.

Sceptics might be wondering, "What's so great about Africa?" Indeed, there are many common misconceptions about this continent, which has been badly maligned for years, and has unfairly suffered a tainted reputation due to some legendary email scams that originated from a localised area. If that's the image of Africa you have in your mind, you'd better brace yourself, because you are in for a big surprise!

Africa—particularly, Sub-Saharan Africa (SSA)—is enjoying a digital revolution. The continent of Africa has established itself as a global leader in information and communications technology (ICT) and is currently home to 7 of 10 the fastest growing companies in the world.[8] Africa's cutting-edge ICT market has shifted its focus to digital, new, and emerging technologies—all of which offer increased efficiency, reduced costs, faster time to market, more customer focus, new services, and openness.

Africa's rapidly advancing technology market plays a vital role in the continent's economic development and is causing many African cities to explode with growth. Nairobi—Kenya's capital city—has already been dubbed the Silicon Savannah. It all started with a nimble mobile banking system that created new market opportunities for startups and digital entrepreneurs. Today, Nairobi has positioned itself as an epicentre for startups, innovation, accelerators, incubator

---

[8] Daily News Reporter. "Africa Offers Fastest ICT Market." Tanzania Daily News, November 16, 2017. http://dailynews.co.tz/index.php/business/54265-africa-offers-world-s-fastest-ict-market. (accessed December 1, 2017)

events, and investor meetings.[9] According to Bloomberg, Nairobi's tech scene could be worth as much as USD 1 billion by 2019.[10]

But Nairobi is just one of many areas expanding because of Africa's booming technology movement, development, and advancement. Hundreds of technology hubs with scores of highly skilled developers and programmers are cropping up all over Africa, with other developing countries using the Silicon Savannah to advance their ICT plans and infrastructure. These tech hubs are capitalising on Africa's tech trend to drive of GDP growth, advancement, value addition and, especially, job creation. Innovators are taking advantage of ICT platforms to push Africa out of poverty and unemployment by absorbing into the labour market large numbers of well-educated, unemployed younger workers under the age of 35.[11]

The continent of Africa, overall, is experiencing robust economic growth, rising foreign investment, and an expanding urban middle class. Together, these trends are creating an internal market on a global scale. Industries like manufacturing, technology and telecommunications, finance and business services, outsourcing, retailing and hospitality are growing rapidly and bringing major changes to cities. The following

---

[9] Moime, Dipolelo. "Kenya, Africa's Silicon Valley, Epicentre of Innovation." Venture Capital for Africa, April 25, 2016. https://vc4a.com/blog/2016/04/25/kenya-africas-silicon-valley-epicentre-of-innovation/. (accessed December 1, 2017)

[10] Mongalvy, Sophie. "Inside the African Tech Hub Rising in Nairobi." Bloomberg, July 29, 2015. https://www.bloomberg.com/news/articles/2015-07-29/inside-the-african-tech-hub-rising-in-nairobi. (accessed December 1, 2017)

[11] Ndemo, Bitange. "How Kenya Became the Cradle of Africa's Technological Innovation." Newsweek, December 27, 2016. http://www.newsweek.com/how-kenya-became-cradle-africas-ict-innovation-534694. (accessed December 1, 2017)

factors are expected to underpin growth of Africa's commercial activities:[12]

- **Sustained Economic Growth**. Economic growth in sub-Saharan Africa (home of some of the world's fastest-growing economies) matched or exceeded 5% for 9 out of the 10 years between 2004 and 2014. And, it is expected to continue to exceed 5% per year until 2020.
- **Favorable Demographics**. Africa's population is currently over one billion and is expected to double over the next 25 years. The working population is experiencing strong growth, with 70% of the total population under the age of 30. This trend in Africa's demographics is making Africa a global scale market.
- **Rapid Urbanisation**. Africa is urbanising faster than any other content. Many African cities are booming, and several are some of the fastest-growing cities in the world.
- **Expanding Middle Class**. The urban middle class is expanding and gaining increased discretionary income due to Africa's sustained economic growth.
- **Commodities and Energy Resources**. Africa's abundant natural resources will continue to fuel global demand for oil, natural gas, and other commodities.
- **Innovation and Technology**. Robust entrepreneurship in many African cities is creating strong performance in multiple

[12] Bradford, Mark. "The 10 African cities poised for take-off." World Economic Forum, May 8, 2014. https://www.weforum.org/agenda/2014/05/top-10-cities-forum-africa-2014/. (accessed November 26, 2017)

innovation sectors—particularly mobile telephony, mobile banking, and mobile technology, in general.

- **Increasing Foreign Direct Investment (FDI)**. FDI volumes in sub-Saharan Africa grew by 41% between 2007 and 2014. China has been making significant contributions to FDI growth as it seeks to tap into Africa's natural resources and back infrastructure development. FDI from developing countries and private equity funds is also growing.
- **Service Sector Growth**. Africa's rapidly expanding internal marking is creating a major demand for personal banking services, business finance, and microfinance. New forms of banking, such as mobile banking, are also emerging.
- **Offshore Jobs**. Africa is a more recent player in the offshoring sector, which has been dominated by India, Central Europe, and Southeast Asia. Nevertheless, Africa's offshoring market has been growing strong in recent years as a result of its low-cost proposition, ready availability of talent, English and French language skills, and favorable time zones for businesses in the Western World.
- **Improving Governance, Economic Management, and Transparency**. Africa's business environments are improving, and economic governance is becoming more rigorous.

- **New Infrastructure, New Cities**. Investment in Africa's infrastructure (particularly, transportation via roads and railways, utilities like hydropower, and telecommunications) is progressively increasing, with China as a major source of funding.
- **Rapidly Evolving Commercial Real Estate Market**. The real estate sector in Africa is young, but experiencing robust development as urbanisation rapidly increases and businesses and consumers place a heavy demand on the industry for a modern real estate structure.

How East Africa compares with other popular offshoring locations:

Certainly, offshoring can be done anywhere; however, in AoteA's extensive experience, East Africa is the best choice. We say this for many reasons, but particularly because 1) the business culture in East Africa is the most closely aligned with that of the Western World; 2) English is spoken with an accent Westerners can easily understand; and 3) East Africa offers a time zone advantage because it's closer to the Western World than other popular offshoring countries.

We believe East Africa compares favorably to most common offshoring locations—like Pakistan, India, the Philippines, Vietnam, and Eastern Europe—in the following ways:

- High degree of staff loyalty and low attrition rates
- High availability of internet and connectivity
- High availability of skilled and talented resources
- Fewer cultural and religious differences
- Less bureaucracy
- Safety when visiting and conducting business
- Price advantage, as well as price continuity
- Political stability

Chapter 3   The Dark Side of Traditional Outsourcing

Your company's reputation is one of its greatest assets, and protecting its good name is always a top priority. Although shielding your company's image from public scrutiny is very important, it's just not enough. You also need to manage how your employees view your organisation from the inside. Keeping your employees happy is key to productivity and helps with retention.

In this chapter, we'll examine some of the ways in which old school outsourcing can tarnish your company. You'll find some of these risks, like layoffs, more obvious. But, outsourcing can also cause problems in more subtle ways that might surprise you. As you'll see, the negative ramifications of outsourcing are varied and serious. However, the good news is that IT offshoring can mitigate all of them.

How Outsourcing Can Create Public Image Problems

The public is typically not keen on hearing that a company has decided to outsource. The general view is that sending jobs abroad will result in layoffs and increase the local unemployment rate. Moreover, the public sees outsourcing as a loss of tax revenues and decreased economic growth.

Naturally, full-time workers start to worry about losing their jobs and begin "jumping ship" as a prophylactic measure. Many times, the employees who leave are star-players, which results in the loss of both know-how and highly desirable talent.

Customers also get worried when they learn an organisation has started outsourcing. This often results in reduced sales and companies losing their competitive advantage. When customers fear their current supplier is having financial problems, they are more likely consider the products or services of a different company.

IT offshoring largely eliminates public image problems and helps retain key employees. We'll tell you how in subsequent chapters.

How Outsourcing Can Make Workplace Morale Plunge

Using foreign workers gives full-time employees the impression they are being replaced by outsiders. This is especially true when companies use third-party consulting firms to hire foreign workers for their onshore facilities. Typically, this type of outsourcing is accomplished through government programs, such as specialised worker visas, which admit a limited number of immigrants into a country each year.

However, there are high costs associated even with these types of arrangements. Many government programs limit the length of time guest workers can stay in their country. The result is an ongoing influx of less experienced workers and the departure of workers who take their know-how with them when they leave. The costs associated with training and integrating these outsourced workers are often significant.

Foreign workers can introduce cultural problems into the workplace:

These days, it's not uncommon for companies to hire large numbers of foreign workers at their onshore facilities. Many IT organisations are currently undergoing a rapid change in their demographics and, in many cases, it is having a deleterious effect on corporate culture and employee morale. Local workers are feeling alienated and disconnected because, in places like hallways, business meetings, and the company cafeteria, foreign workers are speaking languages other than the primary language of the country in which they are working. Consequently, the local workers are finding themselves left out of important discussions and lacking opportunities to interact with their co-workers.

Proponents of this outsourcing model believe it promotes cultural diversity, resulting in a broader range of talent, experience, and perspective. Although this makes sense theoretically, it doesn't always work in practice. For an environment to be truly culturally diverse, the various cultures must accept and appreciate each other's differences. But this is often not the case.

For example, because of India's vast size, its people have diverse religions, customs, and traditions. And, even though the India of today promises equal rights for women, discrimination against women occurs at every stage of life and stems from India's patriarchal culture and customs.[13] India's ancient caste system encouraged the idea that women are inferior and subordinate to men. However, in more modern countries, like the U.S. and much of Europe, women are viewed as equals. So, it's easy to see how these types of cultural attitudes toward women could cause clashes and lower morale in the workplace.

How Lack of Accountability Can Undermine Profitability . . . and More

Organisations are managed from the top down and the decisions leaders make can affect more than just the bottom line. Obviously, the ways in which executives carry out their goals and objectives have a significant impact on a company's finances. But their actions also influence how employees perceive the company and the management team and can have a profound effect on employee morale and individual job satisfaction. Employees expect top-management to be fair and ethical. When they see executives shirking responsibility or

---

[13] "Women's Situation in India," Saarthak Initiatives of Relevance.
http://www.saarthakindia.org/womens_situation_india.html.
(accessed October 23, 2017)

profiting at their expense, workers often become dissatisfied and restless.

Traditional outsourcing has guaranteed job security to undeserving C-suite executives at IT organisations all over the world. By contracting with an outsourcing consultancy, corporate leaders can "pass the buck" and blame the outsourcing firm when projects fail. This way, incompetent executives get to keep their jobs, as they are not held accountable for their failures.

Because IT organisations rarely develop personal relationships with the workers employed by conventional outsourcing consultancy firms, and because those workers never become part of the contracting company's team, execs often feel no guilt about throwing nameless and faceless workers under the bus.

When projects fail, IT organisations will often change partners and hope for better results with a different outsourcing consultancy. But, in the long run, swapping out outsourcing providers slows down progress, limits opportunities for corporate innovation, and erodes a company's competitive edge. It also adversely impacts the bottom line.

Moreover, when employees are not allowed to own their success, it has a negative impact on their morale.

As you'll see later in this book, IT offshoring significantly lowers the risk that a project will fail. In so doing, it either eliminates or greatly decreases the chance your organisation will suffer because of these types of issues.

How Top Outsourcing Firms Perpetrate Abuse on Workers
Third-party consulting firms are notorious for providing poor living conditions for their workers, who are frequently overworked and underpaid. Living areas are often filthy and

situated in undesirable locations. Sometimes small units, like a one-bedroom apartment, are shared by many workers. During the Y2K crisis, it was a common practice to house a large group of programmers in a tiny, grimy room.

Recently, Infosys paid USD 1 million to settle litigation regarding the abuse of visa rules in the U.S.[14] Infosys maintains a large presence in New York State and provides consulting and outsourcing services to many clients in the financial sector and other New York-based industries.

To perform the services Infosys offered, its foreign workers needed U.S. guest worker visas (H1-B). But to avoid the hassle and costs associated with procuring such visas, Infosys knowingly and unlawfully obtained temporary visitor visas (B-1) instead, because the latter are much easier to secure. Holders of B-1 visas are not allowed do the type of work these people were doing. Moreover, the B-1 visa is not subject to the prevailing wage requirements set by the H-1B visa. By misusing the B-1 visa, Infosys was able to pay these New York workers less than what comparable H-1B visa holders would be paid to do the same job. By cheating their workers out of wages, Infosys also cheated the State of New York out of tax revenues.

In addition, the New York State Attorney General's investigation found that Infosys had given its B-1 visa employees instructions on how to lie to U.S. consular officials, customs officers, and border protection officers.

In the U.S., even when employers use the correct guest worker visa (H-1B), fraud is a significant issue. A study

---

[14] "Infosys Pays $1 Million for Work Visa Violations in the US." The Huffington Post, June 24, 2017. http://www.huffingtonpost.in/2017/06/24/infosys-pays-1-million-for-work-visa-violations-in-the-us_a_22894540/. (accessed October 30, 2017)

conducted by the United States Citizenship and Immigration Service (USCIS) in September 2008 concluded that 21% of the H-1B visas issued came from willfully fraudulent applications or those that contained technical violations, errors, or omissions of material facts.[15] Many visa applicants misrepresent their training and skills, often claiming to possess college and university degrees they have not earned. No doubt this kind of fraud is a global problem that affects countries with similar legislation around guest workers.

[15] U.S. Citizenship and Immigration Services. "H-1B Benefit Fraud & Compliance Assessment," September 2008. http://www.uscis.gov/USCIS/Resources/Reports/uscis-annual-report-2008.pdf. (accessed October 21, 2017)

Chapter 4   Navigating Security Vulnerabilities

When operating in a global arena, it's important to have the appropriate defences in place to protect your intellectual property. This means safeguarding your company's databases, software, copyrights, patents, trademarks, designs, and trade secrets from cybersecurity threats.

Before you can even begin to think about establishing your own captive centre offshore, you must be intimately acquainted with the laws and regulations of the country and region where you plan to conduct business. This includes having a complete and thorough understanding of topics such antitrust law; enforcement provisions (for civil and criminal due process); dispute resolution; and, the overall implications for global competition between developed and developing countries in an integrated world market.

In this chapter, we discuss some key areas of legislation you need to be aware of when conducting business abroad. As you'll see, not all countries offer the same protections. In fact, some offer very little or even virtually none.

How IT Outsourcing Can Compromise Your Intellectual Property

The implications associated with intellectual property violations are mind-blowing. These abuses can pose great threats to corporations and sometimes even result in death or injury to their consumers.

Working with a traditional IT outsourcing firm presents many of the same problems you run into when considering a location for your captive centre. You need to know that the outsourcer's service centre is in a country that provides certain measures of protection. But things can still go wrong. There's so much churn that you never really know who is working for you, or who else your workers might be working for. Because traditional outsourcers generally don't have strict vetting processes, you could have criminals on your team and not even know it. Sometimes they hide in plain sight.

The global counterfeiting crisis:

Counterfeiting is one area that's been getting a lot of press lately because it has become a worldwide crisis. Globally respected brands, like Tommy Hilfiger, are constantly fighting and confiscating the goods of counterfeiters who produce fake products that bear the company's logo.[16] But Tommy Hilfiger is just one example of a big-name company that routinely spends millions of dollars on trademark infringement litigation to preserve its brand's image. According to a 2016 report by the Organisation for Economic Co-operation and Development, global trade in counterfeit and pirated goods represented up to 2.5% of world trade, or as much as USD 461 billion.[17] Organized crime syndicates and terrorist groups, like al-Qaeda, are major players in the counterfeiting industry and use the proceeds from the sales of fake goods to fund their operations.

Drugs and medical devices are also routinely counterfeited and distributed globally. According to the Office of the U.S. Trade Representative (USTR), 97% of the drugs seized at the U.S. border in Fiscal Year 2015 came from four Asian economies: China, Hong Kong, India, and Singapore.[18]

---

[16] "Tommy Hilfiger fights back against online counterfeiters." Trademarks & Brands Online (TBO), April, 21, 2017. https://www.trademarksandbrandsonline.com/news/tommy-hilfiger-fights-back-against-online-counterfeiters-4981. (accessed December 5, 2017)

[17] OECD/EUIPO (2016), Trade in Counterfeit and Pirated Goods: Mapping the Economic Impact, OECD Publishing, Paris. http://dx.doi.org/10.1787/9789264252653-en. (accessed December 5, 2017)

[18] Brennan, Zachary. "USTR: 97% of Counterfeit Drugs in US Shipped from Four Countries." Regulatory Affairs Professional Society

Since 2008, INTERPOL's Operation Pangea has been committed to tackling internet sales of counterfeit medicines and educating the public about the danger of buying drugs online. In 2015, Pangea seized a record 10.7 million fake and illicit drugs with an estimated value of USD 81 million.[19]

Regulatory processes in certain countries are either inefficient or virtually non-existent. The internet makes it easy to market fake items, which are virtually indistinguishable from their genuine counterparts. Every day across the world, people are playing roulette by unsuspectingly taking counterfeit drugs, steroids, and hormones to prevent and treat diseases like high-cholesterol, impotence, AIDS, and cancer—as well as bogus nutritional supplements. At best, counterfeit drugs may have none or too little of the active ingredient stated on the label. At worst, some of these items are life-threatening poisons.

According to new research from the World Health Organisation (WHO), an estimated 1 in 10 medical products in low- and middle-income countries is either substandard or falsified.[20] The findings showed the fake drugs and medical products were about equally divided between generic and patented products in every price range. Hundreds of thousands of children die each year, just from pneumonia and malaria alone. The cost to patients and health providers for further care

---

(RAPS), May 2, 2016.
http://www.raps.org/regulatoryDetail.aspx?id=24853. (accessed December 5, 2017)

[19] INTERPOL Operation Pangea VIII.
https://www.interpol.int/Crime-areas/Pharmaceutical-crime/Operations/Operation-Pangea. (accessed December 5, 2017)

[20] "1 in 10 medical products in developing countries is substandard or falsified." World Health Organisation, Geneva, November 28, 2017.
http://www.who.int/mediacentre/news/releases/2017/substandard-falsified-products/en/. (accessed December 3, 2017)

due to failure of treatment runs more than USD 38 million every year. Globalisation is making medical products increasingly difficult to regulate because counterfeiters manufacture and print packaging in different countries, sometimes using offshore companies and bank accounts to facilitate sales.

Clearly, counterfeiting is a serious problem. If your company is in the manufacturing business—whether it's consumer goods, pharmaceuticals, OEM parts, or any other physical products—your brand could be at risk. And, chances are high that a fraudster in an offshore country that offers you little to no protection could make and sell fake versions of your product. This type of criminal activity is easy to get away with in countries that have not yet developed and is often impervious to prosecution.

It's just not worth risking your brand to save a little extra money. In the long run, it could end up costing you a lot more. It would be much safer to partner with an offshore development centre like ours that operates in East Africa where foreign businesses are protected by legislation, carefully vets and certifies all its workers, and lets you choose your own team so you know exactly who is working for you.

Don't trip over TRIPS:

The TRIPS Agreement (Trade-Related Aspects of Intellectual Property Rights)—which is part of the agreement that established the World Trade Organisation (WTO) in 1994—offers universal standards of protection for intellectual property. TRIPS outlines criminal procedures for cases of commercial-scale trademark counterfeiting or copyright piracy.

To date, only 164 countries have signed the Agreement to-date.[21] AoteA is careful to locate its offshore development centres only in TRIPS-compliant countries. In fact, AoteA's current and prospective locations are among the 76 countries that have been on board with TRIPS since it first went into effect on January 1, 1995.

When the TRIPS Agreement was established, WTO afforded less-developed countries (LDC's) special and differential treatment, allowing them additional time to ensure compliance with the possibility of further extensions. In 2013, members of the WTO agreed to extend the deadline for LDC's by eight years, requiring them to implement TRIPS compliance by July 1, 2021.[22] Additional time was granted to allow LDC's to adopt the appropriate laws and policies and develop the infrastructure needed to administer intellectual property protections effectively. Later, in 2015, the WTO committee agreed to extend another waiver, which gives LDC's until 2033 to apply and enforce intellectual property rights on pharmaceutical products.[23]

So, in other words, you should think twice before you choose to locate your offshoring operation in a non-TRIPS compliant country (which probably also lacks other treaties governing intellectual property rights between nations). While the potential for even greater cost savings might seem appealing at first, you could end up losing big, because you

---

[21]World Intellectual Property Organisation (WIPO). http://www.wipo.int/wipolex/en/other_treaties/parties.jsp?treaty_id=231&group_id=22. (accessed December 1, 2017)

[22] World Trade Organisation. https://www.wto.org/english/tratop_e/trips_e/ldc_e.htm. (accessed December 1, 2017)

[23] World Trade Organisation. https://www.wto.org/english/news_e/news15_e/trip_06nov15_e.htm. (accessed December 1, 2017)

would have no protection if something happened to go sideways. Things like counterfeiting, piracy, unexpected political upheavals, changes in a regime, or revisions made to the foreign policy of a state can all have disastrous effects on your global business.

But what about intellectual property rights other than commercial-scale trademark counterfeiting or copyright piracy? When it comes to other types infringements, it's up to the signatories of the TRIPS Agreement to decide whether criminal procedures and penalties should be applied. Infractions are more likely to be prosecuted if they are committed willfully, on a commercial scale. This means that, even if the Agreement is enforced, you still might not recover everything you lost. So, it really pays to choose an offshore partner you can trust. At AoteA, we have done our due diligence. If you choose us as your offshoring provider, you can skip the hassle of scouting out a safe location and get your overseas office up and running quickly.

How to protect your intellectual property:
Nowadays, every company must have an intellectual property protection strategy built into its operating protocols. And, when you go global, it's imperative to be mindful of who you choose as a business partner abroad. To protect your company's assets, you'll want to put security measures in place that restrict how much access your foreign partners can have to your intellectual property.

When doing business in foreign country, it's downright scary how much you need to know about its laws! Working with foreign outsourcing contractors can jeopardise your intellectual property—and, depending on the country, you might have little or no recourse if that happens. But, there's no reason to expose your company to such risks. IT offshoring with AoteA can help put your concerns about intellectual property violations to rest.

How IT Outsourcing Can Compromise Data Security and Cybersecurity

Safeguarding your data and protecting your assets from cybersecurity threats are two of the most important considerations for any organisation, but particularly for those that conduct business overseas.

Between the years 2000 and 2017, the number of global internet users skyrocketed from 360 million to over 3.58 billion.[24] This explosive growth was mostly due to rapid advances in technology, which have made it easier than ever for us to connect all around the world. More users and better accessibility help facilitate doing business globally, but these benefits come with a price: increased cybersecurity risks.

Governing cyberspace is difficult, mainly because there's no universal language around the use of the internet. Technology has developed faster than the global understanding of appropriate norms and values. The larger problem is the lack of universal rules and laws governing the use of the internet, which makes it difficult—and sometimes impossible—to prosecute cyber criminals. The difficulty of enforcing laws is compounded by the fact that cyberspace has no physical borders.

Common types of internet security threats:

Targeted attacks are on the rise. Unless you have robust computer security measures in place, you could fall prey to data breaches, espionage, subversion, and sabotage at any time. Nefarious criminals routinely use email threats, malware, bots, and other types of "mass market" cyberattack tactics to perpetrate offences on a large scale. Vehicles such as email and

---

[24] Statistica. https://www.statista.com/statistics/273018/number-of-internet-users-worldwide/. (accessed December 5, 2017)

malicious web pages can introduce malware to wreak havoc in various ways, such as wiping out data, stealing trade secrets, or even filching personal information from mobile phones.

In the past, ransomware—which locks your data and holds it hostage (or locks you out of your computer) until you pay the ransom demanded—was more likely to be used to target individuals. However, today, the ransomware crime wave is growing, and attacks are rampant.[25] In fact, according to Symantec's 2017 Internet Security Threat Report, ransomware is currently the most dangerous cybercrime threat to both businesses and consumers.[26] Between 2015 and 2016, the average ransom amount extorted from victims shot up from USD 294 to 1,077.

Mass-market cyber criminals have been around for a long time. They take the shotgun approach with indiscriminate mass attacks targeting a great many victims for smaller amounts of money. However, another type of cybercrime has recently emerged. Daring gangs of organised criminals have begun using sophisticated malware campaigns (Trojans) to perpetrate targeted financial heists. The payoffs are often huge. For example, in 2016, a criminal group using a Trojan dubbed Banswift robbed Bangladesh's central bank of US 81 million.[27]

In January of the same year, the Ordinaff group launched a particularly insidious Trojan targeting global

---

[25] Pham, Sherisse. "What is ransomware?" CNN Tech, June 28, 2017. http://money.cnn.com/2017/05/15/technology/ransomware-wannacry-explainer/index.html. (accessed December 5, 2017)
[26] Symantec, Internet Security Threat Report (ISTR), Vol. 22., p. 56. https://www.symantec.com/content/dam/symantec/docs/reports/istr-22-2017-en.pdf. (accessed December 5, 2017)
[27] Ibid.

banking, securities, trading, and payroll sectors—mainly in the U.S., Hong Kong, Australia, and the UK. The latter bears similarities to the infamous Carbanak Banking Trojan, which has stolen more than USD 1 billion from global financial organisations.[28]

The newest such Trojan, discovered in September 2017, is named Silence (after the hacking group behind it). So far, Silence has targeted mainly Russian banks, as well as some Malaysian and Armenian financial organisations.[29]

Data breaches are another type of cybercrime that's been rapidly escalating in recent years. Most of these involve identify theft. In 2016, 1,209 known data breaches occurred and each one stole, on average, close to a million identities.[30] In total, more than 1.1 billion identities were stolen that year— nearly double the number stolen the previous year. The theft of data is the number one cause of data breaches and makes up more than a third of the total; and, over 91% of these types of breaches involve identity theft (which includes the theft of personal financial and personal health information).[31] There is a huge underground economy associated with the theft of stolen personal identity and credit card information where you can

---

[28] Dimitrova, Milena. "Ordinaff Banking Trojan Is in the Hands of Capable Criminals." Sensors Tech Forum, October 11, 2016. https://sensorstechforum.com/ordinaff-banking-trojan-hands-capable-criminals/. (accessed December 5, 2017)

[29] Dimitrova, Milena. "Silence Trojan – the Latest Carbanak-Like Malware Against Banks." Sensors Tech Forum, November 1, 2017. https://sensorstechforum.com/silence-trojan-carbanak-banks/. (accessed December 6, 2017)

[30] Symantec, Internet Security Threat Report (ISTR), Vol. 22., p. 45. https://www.symantec.com/content/dam/symantec/docs/reports/istr-22-2017-en.pdf. (accessed December 5, 2017)

[31] Ibid., p. 48.

buy virtually anything, including online bank accounts, payment cards, various types of gift cards, malware, fake passports, airline tickets, and more.[32] The costs of these products and services range from less than USD 1 to thousands of dollars.

Leading-edge platforms are particularly vulnerable to cybercrime. This includes mobile and cloud apps, and anything that involves broadly shared data.[33] The Internet of Things (IoT)—which is primarily made up of commonly used home devices like routers, DVRs, and cameras—is another rapidly emerging high-profile threat. These threats will continue to increase as the number of IoT devices grows, mainly because the manufacturers of these devices often don't see security as a priority, and their owners typically don't give the devices a second thought after instaling them. IoT devices often have hardcoded user names and passwords that can be difficult or impossible to change, so their owners rarely even bother to try. Plus, many people still make the common mistake of using the same login credentials for all their accounts. These types of factors put IoT devices at high risk. It's easy for criminals to exploit them because they are virtually in plain sight.

Cybersecurity challenges in developing countries:

Cybersecurity in less-developed countries tends to range from poor to downright terrible. The very nature of the Web is to be open, and that openness offers both advantages and drawbacks. Its disadvantages are much greater in developing countries where internet security, protocols, and policies are inadequate or nonexistent. The lack of protective measures, oversight, and enforcement procedures in these areas makes it much easier for cunning cyber criminals to remain anonymous. This means that hackers are more likely to initiate attacks from less-developed countries where it's easier

---

[32] Ibid., p. 51.
[33] Ibid., p. 64.

for them to hide because the risk of detection is low and it's difficult to trace their activities.

Offshoring in less-developed countries poses enormous security risks and makes your company even more vulnerable to cybercrime. Many of these countries can't even protect their own governments from becoming victims of cyberattacks from their more technically advanced adversaries who wage digital warfare against nation-states.[34] So, they certainly won't be able to protect your data or intellectual property.

Legal protections against international cybercrime:

Today, piracy is one of the biggest issues facing organisations that depend heavily on their intellectual property. The meteoric rise in the number of internet users and advancements in Web technologies have escalated the problem to the global level. Having anticipated that the rapidly expanding World Wide Web would introduce new cybersecurity dangers, the World Intellectual Property Organisation (WIPO) adopted the WIPO Copyright Treaty (WCT) in 1996. WCT is a special agreement under the Berne Convention that protects the rights of digital works and their authors. The WCT offers copyright protection for two specific kinds of subject matter: 1) computer programmes; and 2) compilations of data or other material (such as databases) that constitute intellectual creations under the law.

Under the WCT, each contracting member is required to ensure enforcement procedures are available under its law. In so doing, each member extends permission for legal action to be taken against any act of infringement the Treaty covers. Such

---

[34] Frenkel, Sheera. "Hackers Find 'Ideal Testing Ground' for Attacks: Developing Countries." New York Times, July 2, 2017. https://www.nytimes.com/2017/07/02/technology/hackers-find-ideal-testing-ground-for-attacks-developing-countries.html. (accessed December 5, 2017)

action must provide for swift resolutions to prevent infringement, and for remedies to block further infringement.

The EU is taking a tough stance on data privacy:

The EU General Data Protection Regulation (GDPR) is the most important change in data privacy regulation in 20 years.[35] The EU Parliament approved and adopted the GDPR in April 2016, allowing a two-year transition period before requiring the new policy to be in force effective May 2018.

The GDPR applies not only to organisations within the EU, but also to organisations located outside of the EU if they offer goods or services to, or monitor the behaviour of, EU data subjects. The regulation applies to all companies that process and hold the personal data of data subjects who reside in the European Union, regardless of the company's location. By definition, "personal data" is any information related to a natural person that can be used to identify that person, either directly or indirectly. Personal data can be anything from a name, a photo, an email address, bank details, posts on social networking websites, medical information, or a computer IP address.

Penalties for non-compliance will be steep! Organisations can be fined up to 4% of annual global turnover for breaching GDPR, or €20 Million. This is the maximum fine that can be imposed for the most egregious infringements, such as not having sufficient customer consent to process data or violating the core of "Privacy by Design" concepts.

Fines are to be assessed on a tiered basis. For instance, a company may be fined 2% for not having their records in order (article 28), not notifying the supervising authority and

---

[35] The EU General Data Protection Regulation. https://www.eugdpr.org/. (accessed January 15, 2018)

data subject about a breach, or not conducting an impact assessment.

These rules apply to both controllers and processors, which means that clouds will not be exempt from GDPR enforcement.

How to decrease your vulnerability against data breaches and other cybercrimes

Unfortunately, no technology yet exists that can make you 100% resistant to cybercrime. Even big players aren't immune. The Mirai botnet attack in 2016 is a great example of how hackers can knock out major websites. Mirai botnet took down Netflix Inc., Amazon.com, and many other large-scale sites on the eastern coast of the U.S.—even the site of renowned security researcher and journalist Brian Krebs![36]

That said, there's an awful lot you can do to greatly reduce your risk. The top three ways to protect yourself from things like targeted malware attacks, cybercrimes involving data breaches, extortion through ransomware, and piracy are: 1) state-of-the-art security equipment, tools, and policies; 2) careful and attentive monitoring; and 3) choosing your IT offshoring partner wisely. These measures go a long way when it comes to safeguarding your company's hardware and software, data, and intellectual property.

Who you choose to do business with overseas is just as important as the location you choose. Some of the developing countries that offer the best cost saving incentives have the least internet security. According to Webroot, the highest

---

[36] Culpan, Tim. "Attack of the Cyber Drones." Bloomberg, October 24, 2016. https://www.bloomberg.com/gadfly/articles/2016-10-24/watch-that-fridge-attack-of-the-cyber-drones-is-coming. (accessed December 6, 2017)

number of malicious attacks came from IP addresses in the following developing countries in 2016:[37]

- Vietnam (9%)
- India (8%)
- China (7%)
- Russia (4%)
- Ukraine (3%)

Microsoft detected the highest number of threats in Bangladesh, Pakistan, Indonesia, and Egypt, all of which had an average monthly encounter rate of 24% or more during the first quarter of 2017.[38] Obviously, you wouldn't want to put your trust in any of these countries to keep your data and intellectual property safe, no matter how attractive the potential for cost savings might be.

As we keep stressing over and over, a tremendous amount of due diligence is required to establish your own captive centre offshore. Unless your company has unlimited time, money, and resources to scout out the right location, you're better off going with an offshoring provider with a proven track record.

How AoteA Protects Your Security

AoteA specialises in managing Windows servers®, network routers and switches, databases, and operating systems, but NOT in data management. In fact, Federal law specifically prohibits us from operating a data centre offshore. (However, if a customer has processes in place to allow us to

---

[37] 2017 Webroot Threat Report, p. 7. http://src.bna.com/mme. (accessed December 6, 2017)

[38] Microsoft Security Intelligence Report, Volume 22, January-March 2017, p. 15. https://www.microsoft.com/en-us/security/Intelligence-report. (accessed December 6, 2017)

manage their data within their own compliancy, then we would do it.)

Our offshoring model uses technology that keeps clients in control of their own data. We don't keep copies of anything. Our staff works remotely off YOUR systems, using YOUR mirroring and backup strategies. So, unfortunately, we can't help you with backup and restore or disaster recovery.

However, these restrictions have a significant upside: When your offshore IT team has no access to live data, piracy becomes impossible. Your team logs in to your systems using Virtual Private Network (VPN) or Virtual Desktop Infrastructure (VDI). You are the gatekeeper and have total control over what they can see and do. And, our systems let you watch them, either overtly or covertly.

When a client requires quality assurance testing, the offshore staff works only with test data that has been sanitised and obfuscated. There's no personally discernable information because everything has been overwritten.

Chapter 5   The Main Causes of IT Outsourcing Failure

Although outsourcing can be an effective way for a IT organisation to fulfil its labour needs while keeping costs low, a variety of underlying risks can cause traditional outsourcing methods to fail. For example, IT organisations that rely on outsourcers run the risk of downtime, which can happen at critical times. Such dubious accessibility can severely impact productivity and result in large losses of revenue. As we discussed in Chapter 4, substandard security protocols are another serious risk to consider, especially with outsourcing contractors located offshore in foreign countries. If a security breach occurs, customers can find themselves unable to prosecute because the laws of that country offer no protection for intellectual property and other types of private data.

While the above risks are serious and very real, they are not the primary causes of outsourcing failure. When outsourcing bombs, it is usually due to one or more of the following reasons:

- Unrealistic expectations
- Poor communication
- Poor performance
- Conflicting interests
- Negative public opinion

Let's take a closer look at each of these problems and see how IT offshoring either mitigates or eliminates all of them.

Unrealistic Expectations

IT organisations often regard old-school outsourcing as the best way to reduce costs and increase profits. But, in reality, traditional outsourcing is a less than perfect solution because the costs usually end up being higher than planned, eroding profitability. Thus, high expectations are rarely met.

Additionally, to win contracts, conventional IT outsourcing firms commonly overstate the benefits of their services and the competencies of their staff. Outsourcing firms provide unnamed "pools" of technical staff. The individuals in these amalgamated groups remain anonymous to the IT customer contracting the outsourcing services. Outsourcers like to throw junior staff at bigger contracts to train and allow them to gain experience, all at the customer's expense. This can lead to poorly qualified staff working on critical deliverables because the outsourcer sees higher profits from the contract that way. Generally, the amount of collaboration between the technical staff and the customer is minimal.

At AoteA, we allow you to vet and interview your own staff, who remain dedicated to you for the duration of the contract. This way, you can match the type of work you want offshore to the known skill sets and experience levels of your overseas team. If a new skill is required, you can choose to expand your team.

Poor communication

If an outsourcing firm's employees don't understand the customer's goals or deliverables, their work might not measure up to the customer's expectations. Such miscommunications can be very expensive.

Because typical IT outsourcing models contain just a few touchpoints between the customer and the outsourcer, they can produce information black holes. Work disappears into a huge machine, and then later, at a set time, an end-product appears. The level of steering and interaction can vary wildly.

Traditional IT outsourcing models commonly use workers from countries such as India and the Philippines where spoken English is often poor or non-existent. Consequently, all communications must be channelled through a limited number of English speakers whose levels of spoken English can vary hugely. These "translators" often become bottlenecks, and sometimes they even misunderstand what they're told and then go steer developers in the wrong direction. Mistakes like that can be very expensive.

Because AoteA lets you choose your own staff, you know each team member's level of spoken English in advance and can adapt accordingly. For example, the English spoken by graduates in East Africa, where our ODC is located, tends to be extremely high. Their accents are easy to understand because they are much like those heard in the Western World. However, should communication ever break down, we always have native English speakers available to bridge the gap.

Poor performance

It is relatively easy for IT managers to oversee their onsite employees; however, the staff at traditional IT outsourcing firms often operate without direct oversight. Consequently, they sometimes skimp on quality or provide poor service in other ways.

In a traditional IT outsourcing model, the customer passes control to the account manager or project manager within the outsourcing organisation, and that individual ensures that the project is delivered to spec and on time. Obviously, the customer will have review meetings throughout the course of the project, but these reveal only what the outsourcer wants to show. Once the reins have been handed over, the outsourcer can cover up poor quality and slow delivery, citing all sorts of "external factors" that are to blame for the failure to deliver.

With AoteA's IT offshoring model, such a scenario is just not possible. Since your team works as your branch office, they are always connected to your systems. Plus, you have total visibility, so you can monitor what they are doing. You can review ongoing work whenever you wish, and even look at their code while they are writing it. This arrangement helps you identify issues before they become major problems. By providing feedback to your team, you can show them how your processes work and school them, so they become familiar with your organisation's best practices. Unlike traditional IT outsourcing providers, AoteA supplies you with an offshore team that works the way *you* want and uses the same tools you use.

Conflicting Interests

A conflict between the cultures or interests of the customer and the outsourcing firm can lead to failed initiatives. For example, a business that outsources production usually wants its products to have as few defects as possible. However, to gain greater benefits, the outsourcing firm may choose to focus more on quantity without worrying much about quality.

Most IT outsourcing providers look to the bottom line. If the contract says to deliver a product in four weeks, they will do so. But, to keep costs low, they might produce work that has a lot of defects and/or performance issues. Unless the contract is specific about escaping defects, bug counts, performance, and similar issues up front, the customer can be presented with a barely workable solution without any recourse, because the outsourcer has *technically* met the criteria for the contract.

AoteA's IT offshoring model puts you, the customer, in control. You receive a certain number of person-days to use per month, at a fixed cost. We give you the flexibility to stretch this number a little at times to ensure on-time delivery. You get to decide what your priorities are. By creating a product roadmap, you ensure that you are always in control of the time, and of both functional and non-functional features.

Public Opinion

As we mentioned in Chapter 2, the public can have a negative opinion of IT organisations that outsource labour.

Outsourcing is viewed as "sending jobs abroad" and creates an image that can potentially harm a company's reputation. Such an image can easily damage public relations or result in a boycott of the company's products.

By contrast, when you offshore IT work with AoteA, the public views your decision differently. You're no longer seen as a company that's sending jobs overseas. Now, you are "setting up a branch office in East Africa." The public sees this as a positive development. Setting up shop in overseas fosters the idea that the company is prosperous and growing.

Chapter 6   How IT Offshoring Puts You Back in the Driver's Seat

For decades, a cartel of huge and powerful outsourcing firms has been holding their customers hostage. They've been able to keep the price of their services ridiculously high by making it practically impossible for competitors to enter the lucrative IT outsourcing market. And, as you already know from reading earlier chapters, partnering with those providers sharply raises the risk that your project with go south, either because of cost overruns, missed deliverables, poor communication, attrition, or some combination of these or other reasons.

It's time to take back control. And, thankfully, you can. IT offshoring helps you reclaim what traditional outsourcers try to take away. For one thing, you will no longer be a victim of their merciless price gouging. Think you need your own captive centre to enjoy substantial savings? Not true! You can partner with AoteA as your IT offshoring provider. Sure, owning your own captive is cheaper in the long run, but can your company afford to build one? If you read Chapter 2, you already know how much time and money it takes to do that—not to mention the risks involved. Unless you work for a mega corporation that has vast resources, a captive centre is unlikely to be in your future. However, having your own overseas office at an IT offshoring provider's ODC is probably a lot more affordable than you think.

This chapter highlights the ways in which partnering with AoteA puts you back in the driver's seat and headed for the winner's circle. Setting up your overseas development headquarters at our ODC in East Africa is fast and easy. We provide you with a turnkey office, and you have your own dedicated IT staff who work on your projects, using your tools and methodologies. You get to have total control of your how your IT projects are run, which helps ensure that deliverables are on time and work like they're supposed to. You'll soon see that, in both the long- and short-run, partnering with AoteA can save you time, money, and a whole lot of headaches.

You Save On Development, IT, and Infrastructure Costs

Although IT offshoring offers many advantages, cost reduction is still the primary driver. And when you employ overseas workers, the savings in labour costs alone can be very substantial. With AoteA's offshoring model, you can get three or four overseas developers for the price of one in-house. This means you have the potential to get three to four times as much work done for the same price. Talk about a competitive edge!

Additionally, all the costs associated with maintaining your physical office overseas are included in your fixed monthly pricing. We don't bill you separately for floor space, furniture, power, IT equipment, and so on.

You Get a Branch Office with Your Own Dedicated Resources

AoteA provides you with a remote branch office and your own dedicated staff, who work solely with you every day. They join your meetings and scrums. And you can even indoctrinate them into your corporate culture by having them wear your company logo, for example.

Your offshore team is completely dynamic. You may use your resources as you please and assign your staff to projects as you see fit.

When individuals have proven their skills to you and have shown themselves to be loyal and solid performers, AoteA gives them opportunities to progress and improve by taking courses on topics like ITIL or PRINCE2, or specialist technical training.

You can also offer training to your resources yourself. The training can take place at the offshore facility; or, you can have your offshore staff visit your local office for a time and receive their training with you, personally. This teaches them about your work ethics and culture and gives them a better understanding of your environments.

You can even reward your staff with bonuses or incentives. We facilitate the payments but take no percentage. That way, your staff gets the full amount of which you deem them worthy.

When you work with AoteA, you get to choose your own resources. We even name them in the contract. That way, you know exactly who is working for you.

You Can Choose Your Own Staff from a Rich, Stable Talent Pool

At AoteA, we are very proud of the network of contacts we have developed. This network includes our in-house database of candidates, as well as contacts with universities and technical schools, business people, various officials in national and local governments, and even recruiters for the very rare situation when these other avenues may prove fruitless.

We have a strong reputation with the local workforce and we're a known entity to them, so we often have people coming to us seeking jobs they've heard of by word-of-mouth. They know we don't run a sweat shop that takes advantage of people, like many old-school outsourcing firms do. On the contrary, we pay them well—typically, more than the going rates in the local economy—and they get excellent benefits to boot! And, we take good care of them by providing a modern work facility that's comfortable and air-conditioned. Training and advancement opportunities abound, especially for contracts that run a long time. We've found that many East

Africans are attracted to the opportunity to rub shoulders with workers in the West. They regard the ability to consort with their counterparts in the home office as a fringe benefit.

As the continent of Africa is "young," local talent pools are teeming with recent graduates from universities and technical schools. There are also plenty of IT workers with mid-level experience. Our candidates have current skills and are well-versed in the latest technologies. Many of our candidates also have quite a bit of experience in legacy systems because many of Africa's businesses, universities, and government facilities still use old legacy technology.

To ensure our clients get top-notch talent, AoteA uses a high-end testing tool that we pay for on a subscription basis. It allows real, accurate assessment of programming and other IT-related skills. If you want to see a candidate's test results for yourself, you can. This approach is in stark contrast to traditional outsourcing companies that do the old "bait and switch" trick, where you think you're getting X but instead you get Y—and there's always a "good" excuse. When AoteA tells you you're getting a mid-level programmer with C++ skills, that's truly what you get.

The vast majority of time, the onshore team at the home office very much wants to have a say in who gets assigned to the offshore team, for obvious reasons. Sometimes clients like to get down into the nitty gritty of screening and interviewing candidates. Those who prefer less involvement in the hiring process delegate this task to AoteA. They give us a detailed list of requirements, and we get back to them with our recommendations. However, even those who take a less active role in selecting candidates still want to do a "chemistry check" to ensure that each prospective staff member is a good fit. Ramping up is usually a collaborative effort between the home office and AoteA. Jointly, we come up with the chosen team. You can hire as many or as few people as you need.

The most popular old-school IT outsourcing firms are in India, where the job market is very liquid. Consequently, new hires often don't show up for work because they received a better offer somewhere else in the interim. And, because there's so much competition among employers, attrition rates are high. So, existing employees frequently jump ship without notice, leaving clients high and dry. The outsourcing firms must then scramble to fill these positions, typically pulling from a pool of benched workers.

A chief difference between old-school IT outsourcing and AoteA's offshoring model is the idea of a "standing bench." As benched workers are usually those who've been sitting around the longest—and draining the outsourcing company's money while they earn but don't work—they are the first ones shoved onto a client, regardless of whether they're a good fit or not. The needs of the outsourcing company prevail over those of the client.

At AoteA, we don't carry a standing bench, so our clients never find themselves drawn into this predicament. Instead, we go back to the drawing board and recruit ideal candidates from scratch. Although this process may be slower than a standing bench, it ensures our clients get precisely the type of resource they need, and not just some random benched worker we want to put to work.

Unlike India and other liquid markets, employee attrition rates in East Africa are extremely low. Currently, few outsourcing or offshoring providers operate in East Africa. And with the local economies typically somewhat moribund, there seems to be an excess of talent and labour for the available jobs. So AoteA's workers are thrilled to receive new assignments with us and very rarely leave. In the unlikely event of a departure, we try hard to ensure a smooth transition and are usually successful.

You Can Ramp Up Quickly

Whether at home or abroad, teams assigned to new projects must experience learning curves before they can run at full throttle. That said, you can have your AoteA team in place soon after contract signing. Two to four weeks is a typical timeframe for screening candidates and hiring staff. If a project is straightforward, your team can start being productive the first day. For more complex projects, it can take up to a month for a team to reach an optimum level of productivity.

Obviously, the actual amount of time needed to hire a new team member depends on a host of factors, mostly on the client's side (need), but also on the randomness of the labour side (supply). Sometimes a resource can be added lightning fast—for example, if the client needs a junior programmer and we just happen to have three highly qualified ones right in front of us who are ready to start work immediately. Sometimes hiring can take a bit more time—for instance, when a client needs a senior-level Team Leader with 15+ years' experience.

If you use more resource time than expected during a given month and realise you need more staff, it's easy to ramp up. Similarly, if you expect to use less resource time going forward, you can ramp down the following month. (We have an obligation to give our employees one month's notice). Making changes to headcount is easy. Your monthly costs remain fixed for as long as the number of resource hours stays the same. When you add or take away resources, AoteA adjusts your fixed monthly rate accordingly. It's that simple!

You Can Transfer Knowledge in a Variety of Ways

Home office visits are ideal, so we always suggest that our clients pay the labour and travel expenses for one or two of our East African workers to spend several weeks at the onshore location. That way, they can meet the onshore team and learn about the company's culture, processes, and rules and regulations. Then, the worker(s) return to our facility in East Africa and teach the rest of the offshore team what they learned from their site visit. We've found this to be the best way to handle knowledge transfer, hands down.

Sometimes, unfortunately, clients are unable to take this approach due to cost. In these cases, we recommend accomplishing knowledge transfer using several communication mediums, such as video calls, phone calls, teleconferences, email, and various messaging systems.

Occasionally, a representative from the home office might come to our ODC in East Africa to meet with the entire AoteA team. Such visits are typically shorter than those where offshore workers travel to the home office. Some clients like to come see AoteA's offshore facility for themselves. During their visit, they transfer knowledge and provide direction to their offshore staff.

You Don't Have to Babysit Your Offshore Team
AoteA's human resources function manages your overseas team, so you don't have to waste time dealing with petty personnel issues. But we are flexible regarding HR as well and allow our clients to drive the decision-making process.

Sometimes clients prefer to stay on top of human resources issues, especially the "hands on" types who make it clear up front that they expect the offshore team to abide by the same employee handbook as the home office staff. Other clients would rather have AoteA handle the management of the offshore team and ask us to advise them only if issues come up. Ultimately, you can be involved as much or as little as you like.

AoteA's management team oversees our offshore technical staff to ensure projects stay on track and follow each client's desired development processes and protocols. Our senior managers (and the junior managers who report to them) float from one team to another to check on things, help resolve any issues, and interface the home office management team when necessary.

AoteA's management keeps the offshore staff accountable and ensures each worker meets the client's expected level of performance. In other words, we manage your offshore team as if it was a branch office just down the road from the main office in your home country. Most clients have very precise performance expectations for both their home and offshored teams, so we simply help them manage to those standards.

Many clients already have development and IT-support processes in place at their home office and simply need to have their offshore team to follow the same protocols; however, others are less advanced and need some guidance. Fortunately, AoteA has decades of experience and knowledge of all the latest project management methods, such as Agile, ITIL, and PRINCE2. Our consultants can provide advice on best practices and help you implement the most effective development and IT-support processes. If you're offshoring a Service Desk, we can even help you streamline your workflow and capitalize on efficiencies.

You Get to Focus on Your Growing Your Business

While your onshore team focuses on the projects that are the most critical to the success of your business, your offshore team can be performing more routine IT work, like maintaining legacy systems. By offloading the more mundane tasks to you offshore team, you can allow the best and brightest contributors on your home team more time to do the type of work they enjoy. Sure, you can offer them perks like the latest iPhone, better insurance coverage, or a company car—but, those types of things very expensive. And, besides, your star players can negotiate similar incentives elsewhere. Keeping your top performers usually boils down to one thing: making them happy. And nothing makes developers happier than getting to work on new projects using the latest technology. The best part? *This approach costs you nothing*! In fact, you save money!

Here's another way to use your offshore resources: have them develop new applications. This is often a good option when you need to free up the more junior developers at your home office, so they can shift to other projects. Regardless of how you choose to put your offshore team to work, the cost savings will be considerable.

IT offshoring lets you take control of how you use your time. Delegating work selectively to a competent overseas staff can save you a tremendous amount of time. And then, you can use all the time you gain to focus on growing your business and staying ahead of the competition.

You Own the Project
When your home-office IT staff works on a project, you are in control of project management and the finished product—in other words, you own the project. If you happen to have a branch office in another city and your IT staff there works on a project, you own the project. Similarly, when you partner with AoteA and open a branch office at our ODC in East Africa, you STILL own the project. AoteA doesn't make you relinquish control.

By contrast, when you hire an old-school outsourcing firm, they assume control of everything from project management to the finished product. Because you no longer own it, you have no visibility into the project, so you don't know if it's on schedule or not. You typically don't know who's working on it. And, at the end of the process, you are handed a finished product that seemingly came out of a black box.

The difference between offshoring and legacy outsourcing is that, with AoteA, your offshored team is an extension of your organization, just like any branch office. When you outsource the conventional way, you hand off the work to another company and, in the process, lose control, visibility, and ownership of both the project and the finished product.

You Control Data Security

Offshore resources use your systems, processes, and checks and balances. For even greater security, you can grant them access to your systems via Virtual Private Network (VPN) or Virtual Desktop Infrastructure (VDI). Computers are locked down to your standards (for example, USB lock, no internet access, and so on).

If a client requests additional controls—such as key cards to restrict access to certain areas—we can put those in place, too. The cost for such customizations is included in the set-up fee.

You Get Your Product(s) to Market Faster

Offshoring gives you the ability to get your products or services to market faster, to compete better, and to gain a competitive edge. By adding an offshore staff to your existing development teams, you can get projects out the door sooner. Ultimately, a bigger staff may or may not have an impact on a new product roadmap. However, a strong potential to make significant gains most certainly exists, and the implications of these gains can be huge.

Contract Negotiation Is Simple

AoteA has taken the pain and cost out of contract negotiation. Our baseline IT offshoring contract is a straightforward agreement that focuses on two things:

- Describing the way business is to be conducted
- Using simple statements of work to cover your need to add or subtract resources or change the skillsets of your offshore team

Because there's no need to tender for individual projects, continuous negotiations aren't necessary. A single, overarching agreement—balanced in your favor—details the way you and your offshoring provider do business. This agreement is supplemented by individual statements of work and tailored around the type of resources you require at your offshore branch office.

The goal is zero to minimal paperwork for things like scope and deliverables. If, somewhere down the line, you decide you want to change either, all it takes is a simple modification to the contract. No re-negotiation is required. Adding more staff is just as easy.

There are No Pricing Surprises

Our IT offshoring contract establishes a fixed monthly cost for a set number of resources, regardless of how many hours your resources end up working that month. Each resource on your offshore team is scheduled to work 160 hours per month. If you only work that resource for 120 hours, you still pay for 160 hours. However, if that resource works 200 hours that month, you only pay for 160.

We understand that, during crunch time, you might need a resource to work more than 160 hours in one month. Our contract offers the flexibility to do that occasionally. However, if you expect to have a more long-term need for additional hours, you simply add another resource to your team. This ensures your offshore resource is not abused by being forced to work well over 160 hours a month consistently.

Knowing exactly what your pricing will be from one month to the next eliminates surprises on invoices and enables you to estimate costs reliably and successfully, so it's a lot easier to stay within your budget.

Chapter 7   The Global Talent Mobility Advantage

Today, technology-driven change is accelerating rapidly, fueled by the converging trends of hyperconnectivity, data proliferation, and new and merging technologies that allow improved capabilities and faster development cycles. We can now use data in ways that were previously thought to be impossible. At the same time, hardware keeps getting cheaper, smaller, and more efficient; and, it's often available on-demand.

Digitalisation and new technologies have made it possible to expand collaboration all around the globe. Knowledge, trade, technology, capital, and goods and services are more connected than ever. This radically changing global landscape is forcing organisations to operate in a progressively competitive market. Companies that understand the importance of sourcing global talent will be better-positioned for the future. Over the next 10 to 20 years, the success—and sometimes even the survival—of a corporation will depend on its ability to develop an agile global talent mobility strategy. Coupled with the explosive growth of skilled employees from emerging markets, global talent mobility is expected to grow by as much as 50% by 2020.[39] The time to get in on this trend is NOW!

According to a recent annual global CEO survey conducted by Price Waterhouse Coopers, 97% of the respondents said that having the right talent is the most critical factor for the growth of their business.[40] Additionally, 79% of

---

[39] Mullaney, Eileen. "Why Your Organization Needs a Talent Mobility Strategy." The Huffington Post, January 9, 2013. https://www.huffingtonpost.com/entry/why-your-organization-nee_b_2101792.html. (accessed November 15, 2017)
[40] "Talent Mobility 2020: The next generation of international assignments." Price Waterhouse Coopers, 2010.

the CEO's reported plans to change their strategies for managing talent because of the economic downturn. And, 55% said they would look to change their approach to global mobility. As the economy improves over the next decade, the organisations that emerge as leaders will be those that are able to attract, retain, and deploy they key talent globally.

Having access to global talent is particularly important because workers in many developed countries are ageing at an increasing rate while the working population in most developing countries is expected to grow throughout the decades to come. As local talent pools continue to shrink, it will become more and more necessary to rely on global talent. Moreover, in an increasingly global economy, organisations will need to be able to deliver products and services on a global scale. This necessitates having a talent pool that overcomes international borders. A survey of companies in EU countries shows that the development of information and communication technologies further enhances the need for talent mobility.[41]

Emerging markets are creating significant population shifts. For example, traditional business hubs like Paris, London, and Moscow are being dwarfed in population size by Mumbai, Delhi, and Dhaka.[42] The rankings of the largest city economies in

https://www.pwc.com/gx/en/managing-tomorrows-people/future-of-work/pdf/talent-mobility-2020.pdf. (accessed November 25, 2017)

[41] Gera, S., S. Laryea and T. Songsakul. 2005. International mobility of skilled labor: Analytical and empirical issues, and research priorities, HISSRI Working Paper Series no. 2004 D-01, HRDC-ICSSHRC Skills Research Initiative, http://ideas. repec.org/p/wpa/wuwpit/0507004.html (accessed November 27, 2017)

[42] "Talent Mobility 2020: The next generation of international assignments." Price Waterhouse Coopers, 2010. https://www.pwc.com/gx/en/managing-tomorrows-people/future-of-work/pdf/talent-mobility-2020.pdf. (accessed November 25, 2017)

the world are expected to change drastically by 2025. As these areas grow, so will their talent pools; and new talent pools will emerge as well. This trend will produce a younger and much larger global workforce with a wider variety of talents and skills. The rapidly expanding pool of global talent, together with the upcoming advances in digital and new technologies, will increase the need for organisations to devise more complex global talent mobility strategies.

The Evolution of Global Talent Mobility Through the Eras

The ways in which companies move talent around the world have changed drastically over the past 50 years.[43] From 1970 to 1990, international assignments were piloted chiefly by large multinational corporations based in the U.S. and Europe. These organisations typically sent talent from the country where the company was headquartered into the field to manage overseas operations. In the years between 1990 and 2010, the demand for global talent mobility rose as new markets for products and services emerged, and as manufacturers sought to lower their production costs.

As offshoring gained steam, a new type of mobile worker emerged alongside the expatriate of the previous era. This new breed met the increasing demand for globalisation through commuter, rotational, and technology-enabled virtual assignments. Although talent still flowed mainly from West to East, companies started to venture into emerging markets with rich talent pools—especially, India. As we approach 2020, the mobility of talent is becoming more fluid as it continues to grow rapidly. New technologies will enable organisations to identify and connect with talent virtually instantaneously. In other words, talent mobility will become the new norm as the world becomes increasingly connected and international borders become more blurred.

_____

[43] Ibid.

Offshoring to Gain Access to Talent, Drive Down Costs, and More

To succeed in today's aggressive environment, organisations must consider cost reduction as a key factor in their business strategy. One very effective way to save money is by lowering the costs of labour and overhead, which represent a large portion of an organisation's budget. Large, multinational companies have long had the ability to deploy their talent around the world to make sure they had the right staff in the right place at the right time. A rapidly increasing number of corporations are building their own captive centres, so they can offshore technology functions and business processes. The advantages are tremendous. For one, the cost savings from a captive is potentially at least 35% lower than working with traditional third-party outsourcing service providers.[44]

Although the savings are impressive, driving down costs isn't the only critical strategic objective companies have in mind when they set up their own offshore technology hubs. Captive centres have access to large, highly skilled IT talent pools and can attract better talent with lower attrition rates as compared to outsourcing providers. With more and more companies setting up offices around the world, the global talent war is ON, and will continue to be the key human resource issue until 2020, when the people pipeline appears to be the most critical variable separating the winners and losers in the marketplace.[45]

---

[44] Raju, Adithi and Gupta, Vaibhav. "The Rise of Global In-House Centers: A Case Study Approach." Medium. https://medium.com/@zinnov/the-rise-of-global-in-house-centers-a-case-study-approach-eaf396fee09d. (accessed December 11, 2017)

[45] "Talent Mobility 2020: The next generation of international assignments." Price Waterhouse Coopers, 2010. https://www.pwc.com/gx/en/managing-tomorrows-people/future-of-work/pdf/talent-mobility-2020.pdf. (accessed November 25, 2017)

How Smaller Organisations Can Capitalise on Offshoring

Until recently, smaller organisations with more limited budgets have been unable to take advantage of the cost savings, global talent pools, and two-way transfer of knowledge, skills and experience that offshoring provides. Having access to global talent is particularly important because workers in many developed countries are ageing at an increasing rate while the working population in most developing countries is expected to grow throughout the decades to come. As local talent pools continue to shrink, it will become increasingly necessary to rely on global talent.

At AoteA, we have made it possible for smaller, forward-thinking companies to upgrade their business tactics and strategies. You can now capitalise on all the benefits of IT offshoring without the hassle and expense of building, outfitting, and maintaining your own captive centre. We provide you with a turnkey, remote branch office at our facilities in East Africa. In a way, this is like getting an "office in a box" that's already set up and ready to go, except for the staff, which you choose yourself. You get to recruit your own resources from our vast pool of highly skilled, certified global talent. That way, you can ensure that each person on your team has the experience and skillset you need. The IT professionals you hire are dedicated to you, specifically. So, they are never dividing their time to serve multiple clients, like the way the employees who work for traditional outsourcers do. And security is never an issue because your overseas staff uses YOUR systems, YOUR processes, and YOUR standards. Plus, you get to control each person's level of access and monitor everyone's work in real time.

In today's increasingly competitive market, it's critical to offer exciting career opportunities to attract and retain the best talent. IT offshoring gives you an edge because you can recruit the best people for the job. And, your onshore employees will be a lot happier, too. Because when you offload the more routine IT tasks to your offshore branch office, you free up the developers at your home office so they can do the creative work they enjoy and generate new ideas to help your company stay competitive. This not only allows your company to focus on bringing more innovative products and services to market, but also helps you retain your star players. Good people tend to stick around when their job satisfaction is high and they know their employer can offer them plenty of opportunities for career advancement.

Chapter 8   The Top 10 Disadvantages of Traditional IT Outsourcing

Traditional IT outsourcing is riddled with risks and has many drawbacks. The good news is, the new offshoring model mitigates or eliminates all these shortcomings. Here are the top ten disadvantages we see with old-style outsourcing models.

It Can Ruin Your Company's Reputation

Your company's reputation is on the line, and you need to do everything you can to preserve it.

When you use traditional IT outsourcing, the in-house team is often completely replaced by the outsourcing contractor's team. This gives the impression that your company is laying off its entire local IT staff. Once word gets out, bad publicity can damage your company's name.

By contrast, offshoring lets you keep your core team and supplement it with lower-cost offshore resources. Smaller companies and non-profits, particularly, rely on offshore cost savings to help them grow despite tight budgets.

Data Security Vulnerabilities

When you contract with a traditional outsourcing firm, the resources belong to the outsourcer, *not you*. Will they remain loyal? Will their computers and systems be locked down? Might they use external storage devices for personal purposes?

All these issues can result in data tampering. And, if your data is copied or removed, you may have little recourse because certain foreign countries have no legislation to offer protection for your intellectual property.

When you contract with AoteA, not only do your resources work exclusively for you, but they work remotely off your systems and have no access to real data.

Contract Negotiations are Horrendous

Traditional IT outsourcing firms are notorious for insisting on a baseline contract that requires massive amounts of paperwork. They want to protect their own interests, so they deploy legislation-wrap around the contract.

You want to optimise this relationship, so initial negotiations can be tedious, lengthy and challenging. Dealing with scope creep—which happens frequently as projects unfold—is a nightmare because contract modifications are time-consuming. Changes mean more money, more negotiations, and project overruns.

AoteA blows away the old-school outsourcing companies by offering a baseline one-year contract, whereas the others typically require three- to five-year contracts. A typical outsourcer's contract resembles *War and Peace*. By comparison, our Master Services Agreement is only 18 pages long and is written in plain English, not "legalese."

We are confident that our offshoring service model is the best in the business. That's why we offer our clients the option to cancel their contract at any time for any reason with no penalty or fee. So, if you'd like to try a small pilot programme/beta test before going "all in," you can do so with no obligation to finish out the year.

It's Not Always Cheaper

The biggest allure of traditional IT outsourcing is that, on paper, it appears to offer significant cost savings. But, invariably, costs end up being higher than you expected.

Sure, IT outsourcing sounds good because the hourly labour rates of foreign workers are much lower. But then, the invoice arrives and there are surprises, such as a dramatically higher number of hours worked than expected—plus, sky high contract modification fees for scope changes. This makes it extremely difficult to manage the project, estimate costs, and stick to a budget.

With AoteA's offshoring model, your monthly costs are fixed, so you never see unexpected charges on your bill. If you need more or fewer resources, it's easy to ramp up or ramp down. All it takes is an email or a phone call to make changes, and we'll adjust your contract and monthly costs accordingly.

No Continuity of Resources

When you work with a traditional outsourcing contractor, their resources don't belong to you. So, when projects end, teams get swapped out, resulting in a significant amount of knowledge lost. This means you'll need to retrain the next project team, which costs time and money.

In addition, many countries have policies governing how long outsourcing contract employees must wait before they can be rehired. A three-month waiting period is common. Because of these types of restrictions, you could lose key contributors during a critical time.

At AoteA, we let you choose your own resources from our highly skilled IT talent pool. Each person you hire is named in your contract. You get acquainted with them personally, just like you know your onshore employees. There are no time limits or waiting periods, so you can keep an employee on as long as you like. If you finish one project and start another, you can migrate your whole team over to the new project. That way, your resources retain the knowledge they acquired while working for you. As they gain more experience, their value increases. Over time, your offshore team members can become significant assets to your organisation.

Incidentally, unlike old school outsourcers, we never split our workers' time between clients. The resources you hire are assigned to you *exclusively*. That way, they can be dedicated to YOUR projects and loyal to YOUR organisation.

Time Zone Challenges

Most traditional IT outsourcing contractors use workers in India, the Philippines, and other countries in the Far East. Usually, these locations are far away from the customer's home office, off in a distant time zone. Being separated from their overseas team by such a great distance often creates lengthy delays and communication challenges for IT customers based in the Western World.

Although outsourcing contractors do offer shift work, it nearly always comes with a hefty price tag that greatly lessens the cost savings that drew you to outsourcing in the first place.

In addition, outsourcing forces you to work around foreign holiday schedules which may be different from your own. The unavailability of foreign workers often results in lengthy delays that waste your time and can lead to significant lost revenue.

By contrast, AoteA can offer you service 24/7/365, if that is what you need. You can choose to have all your resources work the same shift or spread them across up to three shifts for 'round the clock coverage.

Communication and Language Barriers

Many traditional IT outsourcing contractors tout the English language skills of their workers. But, there's a big difference between being able to pass a written English language skills test and being able to converse fluently with native English speakers. Even when someone is conversant in English, accents and cultural barriers can impede accurate, efficient communication. This leads to frustration for both your local staff and the outsourcer's IT team.

At AoteA, we select our resources very carefully and only offer you the best. In addition to having the appropriate technical skills, each member of our talent pool is proficient in both written and conversational English. Moreover, our resources are easy to understand because their accents are similar to those heard in the Western World.

You Can't Choose Your Employees

Because of the impersonal nature of traditional IT outsourcing, you have no control over which workers get assigned to your projects. Remember, IT outsourcing contractors like to insert junior people into large projects to give them the opportunity to acquire experience. That means some of the workers assigned to your project may lack basic training or skills. Can you really afford to have a newbie on your team? Perhaps even more importantly, can you afford to be getting a newbie when you're paying for an experienced professional?

At AoteA, we allow our clients to be involved in the hiring process as little or as much as they want. Hands-on types prefer to do their own screening, interviewing, testing and hiring. At the opposite end of the spectrum are those who feel that we are better qualified to choose the resources that will make up their offshore team. Most clients fall somewhere in the middle.

Poor Quality Services

One of the biggest complaints about traditional IT outsourcing is poor quality of service. This problem is due to several factors—primarily, constant turnover, double-dipping, and resources simply moving on to greener pastures.

As we mentioned earlier, outsourcing consultancies often treat their workers poorly, pay them low wages, and house them in deplorable conditions that are dirty, unhealthy, and unsafe. Often, these firms work the same resources on double-shifts to service two different clients at the same time. (Of course, they vehemently deny that they do this.) It's little wonder, then, that tired and mistreated workers produce substandard deliverables.

By contrast, AoteA's workers receive higher pay than most local employers offer, good benefits, a stable working environment, good working conditions, and many opportunities to learn new skills and technologies. We have a great reputation in the East African community and attract some of the best talent. Because our workers are happy, we don't see the churn and high turnover rates that are so typical among those old-school outsourcing firms.

Unprofessional Workers with Substandard Skillsets

One of the most common complaints we hear about old-school IT outsourcers is "bait and switch," whether intentional or not. In other words, they promise you one thing, but give you another. For example, outsourcing firms often allow job applicants to self-certify their own skill sets and experience levels. And, on the rare occasions when they do administer tests, they are usually rudimentary and ineffective because the testing practices are so poor. Consequently, you often end up with a team that lacks the professionalism and skill sets you were promised—and that you are paying for!

With AoteA, you get to choose the team that suits your needs—exactly. We often recommend that our clients choose their team leaders and then allow the team leaders to choose the remaining staff. AoteA's goal is to help you customise your team to *your* requirements. Unlike old-school outsourcing companies, we don't try to shoehorn people into a role from a bench.

Our workers are certified, having passed rigorous technical skills tests. They are proficient in written and conversational English and have the experience levels you

78

require. If you need a mid-level programmer with C++ expertise on your team, that's precisely what you get.

Chapter 9   The Top 10 Advantages of IT Offshoring

IT offshoring with AoteA offers abundant advantages over conventional IT outsourcing. Here are the top 10 ways in which our IT offshoring model is superior.

1. No Real Estate

The cost of desk space is a big consideration. The price per square foot in any major city in the world is a significant factor in the overall cost of providing for an onshore employee. Each employee needs a desk, a chair, a computer, and so on. On top of all that, it takes time to find the right space, negotiate the lease, and build out the space. Plus, you need to be comfortable taking on the long-term commitment. All these things can slow you down.

Our IT offshoring model enables you to set up a development office offshore without paying the high-rents associated with onshore offices. And, you're not required to take on a multi-year commitment, either.

2. Top-Notch Talent

At AoteA, we thoroughly test and certify all our candidates before we employ them. This eliminates one of the most common complaints about outsourced workers. The testing is performed professionally using leading-edge tools like Codility. These tools go beyond simple testing and allow you to see the job applicant's written code. This way, you get what you pay for, which is only fair.

Additionally, our offshore workers are truly fluent in both conversational and written English. They have accents and a cultural background that is as close as possible to that of the Western World.

In sum, AoteA offers you highly talented workers who produce high quality deliverables. Working conditions, pay levels, and managerial practices result in happy, loyal, and productive workers who seldom leave. In the end, you will have a high-performing branch office at a fraction of the cost of your local office.

3. Time Zone Advantage

Our IT offshoring model eliminates the time zone challenges associated with conventional outsourcing firms, which are typically located in Asia and the Far East. Your offshore resources will be in East Africa, which is much closer to the Western World. Need your workers to cover different shifts? Not a problem! You can have offshore staff available all day, every day, if that's what you require.

Smart companies like Google have solved the time zone problem by creating a 24-hour development cycle. This speeds up the process considerably. Such a strategic approach becomes especially important as more and more organisations adopt the Agile Software Development Life Cycle (SDLC) project management methodology, which offers an iterative approach to the design and development of software. Agile embraces the constant changes that occur during development, allowing teams to break down into smaller segments the normally lengthy phases, like building and testing. Ultimately, software can be developed more quickly and released more frequently.

Having two teams of developers—one onshore and one offshore—allows development efforts to continue even though one of the teams have finished their day. The process speeds up considerably when the project is handed off from one team to the next. Some additional management time and coordination between teams are necessary, but the results are staggeringly impressive. A task that would normally take three days using a resource in a single time zone can now be completed in one day with resources who work 'round-the-clock.

4. Eliminates HR and Employment Legislation Hassles

IT offshoring with AoteA frees up your human resources staff by cutting out the need to write job postings, prescreen applicants, and interview A-list candidates. We manage all these tasks for you. And, here's another bonus: You don't need to slog through reams of red tape to get approvals for job sites, salary levels, and various other details.

You establish your budget with us up front, and the cost counts as a regular business expense. There's no need for you to manage employee payroll or benefits. Nor will you need to worry about HR issues if someone needs to be released from the team.

Another detail you don't need to worry about is foreign legislation pertaining to things like owning office facilities, employment, data security, and protection of your intellectual property. Keeping up with the laws in foreign countries can be a nightmare. Frequently, you don't even realise you need to be aware of something until you run into it—and, by then, it might be too late. The consequences to your business can be dreadful. The good news is, offshoring with AoteA eliminates all these concerns.

5. More Time to Focus on Projects

AoteA manages your offshore team, so you can avoid the headaches associated with managing people located halfway around the world. Your overseas team works for a single organisation that handles all the basics like ensuring each of your employees arrives on time and puts in a full days' work. You can sleep soundly knowing that someone is watching over your team and generating reports you can review the next morning. Because you're not wasting time on trivialities, you can focus on the projects your team is working on and help them with any challenges.

6. Responsiveness and Scalability

When you choose AoteA as your IT offshoring provider, we make it easy to change your workforce as your needs change. If you need to increase or scale down resources, all you need to do is pick up the phone or send us an email saying you require more or fewer. There's no need for you to manage office space, infrastructure, or employee termination processes because we do all those things for you.

Furthermore, should a certain resource not work out, you can easily replace them with another. Remember, your relationship is with us, and not with individual resources.

7. Security, Control, and Confidential Information

Modern technology makes it easier than ever to control security and protect confidential information. As we said in Chapter 4, AoteA's IT offshoring model makes it simple to set up Virtual Private Network (VPN) or Virtual Desktop Infrastructure (VDI) access to your current framework. This gives you complete control over access to your systems. You can even instal monitoring software that lets you check in on workers to observe what they are doing. This can be done either covertly or overtly.

8. No Hidden Costs

When you go with a traditional IT outsourcing firm, you often incur additional costs as a project unfolds. Scope creep is common because changes are made routinely as a product moves through the various stages of development.

When you choose AoteA for your IT offshoring needs, you get a dedicated team of resources for a fixed monthly price. This way, scope creep becomes a non-issue. Because there are no hidden costs, you never get blindsided by unexpected charges.

9. Continuity

When you hire a development team through us, we dedicate that team to you *only*. Over time, you develop personal relationships with individual team members. As you get acquainted, you discover their strengths and abilities. Ultimately, you come to know them as people you can count on and trust, just as you have confidence and faith in your home team.

It's a well-known fact that indoctrinating employees into your company's culture leads to better outcomes.[46] AoteA lets you assimilate your offshore team into your organisation. That way, the team can fit in with your corporate culture, wear your company logo, and so on. They become your employees. They know your standards and understand your goals and objectives.

10. Retention Tool for High Performers

Highly paid superstar developers are keen on working with leading-edge technology, playing with the latest "toys," and coming up with innovative solutions. Generally, they detest supporting legacy systems, clearing up technical debt, using tools they consider outdated, and working on tasks and projects they find unchallenging or mindless.

If you've been around developers for a while, you know they'd be happy all the time if only they could focus solely on doing what they love. So, offloading tasks like the maintenance

---

[46] Bradt, George. "Why You Must Make Culture the Centerpiece of Your Onboarding Program." Forbes. October 28, 2015. https://www.forbes.com/sites/georgebradt/2015/10/28/why-you-must-make-culture-the-centerpiece-of-your-onboarding-program/#6b993c151f90. (accessed November 1, 2017)

of legacy systems would give them more time for work they enjoy, right? Theoretically, yes—but, contracting with a traditional IT outsourcing provider often creates more problems than it solves. In fact, it is likely to be a disaster. The constant churn and turnover in personnel will result in inefficiencies, mistakes, and higher costs than necessary or expected. Outsourcing firms are continuously swapping out workers and getting their replacements up to speed burns up a lot of hours.

By contrast, AoteA's IT offshoring model has none of these problems. Because having an office at our ODC in East Africa is just like having your own overseas branch office, there isn't any churn or turnover. In fact, each worker is even named in your contract.

By offshoring the type of work your senior developers regard as banal or tedious, you increase the drive and loyalty of your top contributors. When these developers are no longer required to spend time doing things like fixing trivial issues in a programming language they view as being antiquated, they can focus more on creative work, R&D, prototyping, and other projects that motivate high-performers. The best and brightest get to work on things they love and devise innovations that give your company an edge over the competition. And, when your top-notch developers are happy, they are much less likely to pursue opportunities elsewhere.

In addition, by offshoring with us, you can greatly reduce the cost to support and even continue feature development for legacy systems. Costs for minor, trivial work are low.

So, in this respect, IT offshoring with AoteA is advantageous in two ways: It helps you save money *and* retain your most highly valued developers.

Chapter 10   The Top 10 FAQ's About Offshoring

If you've read this far and still have questions, or if you "cheated" and skipped ahead, this chapter is for you. At AoteA, we encourage people to ask a lot of questions. Now, we'd like to get started answering some of yours by sharing our customers' top 10 most frequently asked questions. Here they are, in no particular order.

1. Isn't IT offshoring risky?

Offshoring is, in fact, **much less risky** than traditional IT outsourcing. At AoteA, we specifically designed our offshoring model to mitigate or eliminate virtually all the risks typically associated with outsourcing. When you send IT work to your offshore branch office at our ODC in East Africa, you get to focus on growing your business instead of managing outsourcing problems.

In a nutshell, these are the key ways in which IT offshoring with AoteA mitigates risk:

- Contract negotiations and modifications to existing contracts are greatly simplified.
- You get a branch office with resources who work only for you 24/7/365, and whom you can integrate into your corporate culture.
- You own your own projects.
- You control the security of your data.

In the end, you win because you get your products to market faster than your competition.

2. How do we know your overseas resources are adequately trained?

Our IT offshoring model has a formal process with strict rules for hiring employees. Traditional outsourcers often have lax hiring policies and allow workers to self-certify their skills. By comparison, our offshore developers need to pass rigorous technical tests. They must also be fluent in both spoken and written English and have accents similar to those of Western World speakers.

In addition, you get to vet the members of your offshore team personally. And, should someone not work out as planned, you can replace that person with a resource who better suits your needs.

3.   *Do your overseas resources have experience in <insert specialised skill here>?*

The testing methods we use to certify offshore workers are highly professional and employ cutting-edge tools to assess workers' skill sets and key competencies. One such tool is Codility, which objectively measures the applicant's computer programming skills. You can even review the applicant's written code personally, to make sure it meets your high standards.

4.   *What if we need to make a change after the contract is signed?*

No problem! Unlike outsourcing contracts—which sometimes rival the size of a phone book for a small city—our contracts are simplified and straightforward. It's easy and painless to modify your contract if, for example, your project runs into scope creep. Or, if you need to increase or decrease the size of your team. All you need to do is pick up the phone or send an email to let us know your needs have changed. Your monthly charges will then be adjusted accordingly, and all the services you need will be included in the new fixed price. You'll never find any hidden costs or surprises on your invoice!

5.   *Will your overseas resources' holidays conflict with our project schedule?*

Foreign holiday schedules can indeed be a problem with outsourcing. Not so with when you contract with AoteA as your

IT offshoring provider! For non-critical assignments, like development, we must honour local holidays. However, if you need your team to operate on a shift schedule that overlaps your time zone, or to provide support 24/7/365, it can be arranged. For 24x7 services, we negotiate with the teams to ensure coverage is met. Vital projects need not be derailed by interruptions in service due to holiday schedules overseas.

6. How can we protect our intellectual property?

Offshoring with AoteA guarantees the security of your data and intellectual property in ways that traditional IT outsourcing cannot. For one thing, your offshore resources belong to *you*, not the provider. You have complete control over access over your systems and the ability to monitor offshore workers, either overtly or covertly. It's very simple to lock down your systems and data by setting up Virtual Private Network (VPN) or Virtual Desktop Infrastructure (VDI) access to your current framework.

In addition, with AoteA, you never need to worry about issues with foreign legislation which, in some countries, offers no protection for your data or intellectual property.

7. How can we be sure your overseas resources aren't being underpaid or mistreated?

It's no secret that conventional IT outsourcing firms are notorious for treating their workers unfairly, paying substandard wages, forcing them to work double shifts, and cramming them like sardines into dreadfully dirty and hazardous housing facilities. This results in exhausted, ill-treated employees who produce second-rate work. Not surprisingly, high employee turnover rates are a major problem. And, one of the worst things about churn is that workers take their knowledge with them when they go.

By contrast, our offshore resources receive better than average salaries and ongoing training. They are offered significant incentive schemes, work in modern offices, and live at home comfortably. The result is happy workers who consistently produce high-quality deliverables.

8. How can we address our customers' and employees' concerns about layoffs?

Traditional IT outsourcing can risk your company's reputation, but offshoring preserves it. When you say you're "outsourcing," people think you are sending jobs abroad because your company is struggling financially and desperate to cut costs. To the public, it looks like you want to replace your home team with foreign labour to avoid paying the higher salaries of the local workers, who will inevitably end up getting laid off. This is a sure recipe for bad press.

On the other hand, when you offshore IT work to our ODC in East Africa, it gives people the impression that your business is booming and expanding, because your company has set up an overseas branch office. The message here is very different: In this scenario, the public views you as supplementing your onshore team with an offshore team, and not replacing the home office staff completely with cheap foreign labour.

9. If we start offshoring IT work, won't we risk losing our best and brightest developers because they will fear they might lose their jobs?

Quite the contrary! Our IT offshoring model helps you retain your top talent. How? Because by offshoring the type of tasks senior developers tend to loathe—like supporting legacy systems or fixing trivial programming bugs—you free up their time, so they can focus on the cutting-edge technologies, creative projects, and "toys" they love and thrive on. When your star players are content, motivated, and absorbed in their work for the sheer joy of it, they are unlikely to seek greener pastures.

10. Does IT offshoring cost more than traditional outsourcing?

No. In fact, our customers are usually surprised to discover our prices are much lower than they expected. Much of the savings is directly related to the cost of resources. Traditional outsourcing firms can have astronomical profit margins, sometimes marking up their rates by 500% to 1,000% and charging the same rate for all resources across the board, regardless of their skills and experience levels. With AoteA, you participate in selecting your own staff and each person you hire is named in your contract. You pay only for the skills and resources you need.

Chapter 11   Case Studies and Examples

In this chapter, we share some case studies and give you various examples based on real customer experiences.[47] The purpose of these sample scenarios is to

- Illustrate various IT offshoring models
- Show you the types of results you can achieve
- Reveal a way to get even better outcomes

As AoteA specialises in supplying offshore IT teams to assist with development, service desk, and network operations centres, we have focused our examples on those areas.

What Kind of Work Should You Send Offshore, and Why?

We hope the case studies and examples in this chapter will inspire you to think of ways you can use IT offshoring to help your business grow. Before jumping into specifics, let's take a moment to get the creative juices flowing by reviewing some possibilities.

Because AoteA's talent pool is so large and diverse, covering a wide range of skills and abilities, you can transition virtually any kind of IT work to your overseas team in East Africa. Typically, organisations choose to offshore the following types of activities:

_____

[47] To protect our customers' privacy, we have chosen not to name specific companies or disclose their home office locations.

- Development
- Maintenance (particularly, of legacy systems)
- Quality assurance testing
- Application production support
- IT infrastructure support

What can you gain by offshoring? Well, it really depends on what your goals are. Here are some common reasons why an organisation might choose to shift IT work to an overseas office:

- Improve the bottom line by drastically reducing IT costs across the board
- Stretch their IT budget by using the cost savings to finance a new IT initiative
- Reduce onshore headcount by a certain number
- Offshore a certain dollar amount of IT costs
- Free up the onshore staff to work on more important projects
- Close an onshore facility

Ever wish you had a bigger IT budget so you could get more done? Who hasn't! The good news is, you can accomplish a lot more with a lot less. Imagine getting three or four developers for the price of one. Yes, it's possible! All you need is an effective IT offshoring strategy. At AoteA, we have decades of experience advising clients. Just tell us your requirements, and we'll make some recommendations and help you come up with a customised plan. For more information about our customised solutions, see Chapter 12.

What Might a Typical Offshore Team Look Like?
The short answer is, it can look like whatever you want it to look like!

Okay, so that's probably not the answer you were expecting, nor is it particularly helpful. What we are trying to say here is that AoteA helps you build an offshore team that's custom-tailored to your needs. You get the exact number of resources you want with precisely the skills you require.

Still not specific enough? Okay, here's an example. Suppose Company X needs to supplement their onshore development staff with a team of offshore developers. Let's further suppose this company has three senior developers at their home office, and each one is leading a separate project, so there are three project streams altogether. To maximise cost savings, the company wants most of the development work to take place offshore, under the direction of the three onshore development leads. The most logical solution for this scenario would be to assign an AoteA development team to support each project stream. Each of the AoteA teams would consist of a lead developer (who would coordinate the offshore work and report directly to the corresponding onshore development lead) plus some combination of developers and programmers having various levels of experience (as needed), and probably a QA tester or two.

So, are you ready to see some offshoring examples based on real customer experiences? Bet you were starting to wonder if we'd ever get to them, weren't you? Well, here you go!

Example 1: Development of a Cheque Clearing System

A conglomerate of banks in a certain country needed to develop a new system for clearing cheques. Since the application was to be used by multiple, competing banks, they created a syndicate to develop the specifications and then went to tender with multiple outsourced development suppliers. This meant no one party owned the intellectual property or the software. Nor did any party gain significant advantage over any other by developing the software in house. Because the specifications committee had a single supplier develop both the software und underlying hardware solution, the systems worked better together.

Example 2: Development of a Gaming Product Line

A large tech company that develops its own gaming platform wanted to create a new product line. Space was at a premium in their current offices, so the company had two options. They could either outsource or open a new branch office. The company chose to open an office – in Hungary. Here's how their plan worked out:

- Time from decision to selection of an office site: 6 months
- Time to outfit the office: 3 months
- Time to recruit (they couldn't begin until they had an office for people to sit in): an additional 3 months
- Cost: Over 500K EUR up front to outfit the office and recruit the first 40 staff members

Ouch.

This company would have enjoyed a much better outcome, more efficiencies, and a greater cost benefit if, instead of opening their own offshore office in Hungary, they had chosen to offshore their IT work to our ODC in East Africa. Here's the AoteA advantage they missed out on:

- Time from decision to getting the first staff online: as little as one month
- Upfront costs: an initial set-up fee plus the cost of one month's contract

Yes, really, **that's it!** Inside of a month, the set-up fee would have covered recruitment costs, time, communications upgrades, and any work needed for security and VPN set up.

Instead of hiring the whole team at once, we would have added staff incrementally, so as not to overwhelm the home office. But even with the slower, staged ramp-up, the team would have had been online sooner, and *at a fraction of the cost* of an office build. Plus, our ongoing fees would have been *significantly* less per capita.

This company's unfortunate experience underscores how important it is to do your homework. Yes, they ended up with their own captive centre in Hungary, but at what price? Their start-up costs were steep, and their ongoing personnel and infrastructure costs will be much greater than the cost of contracting with AoteA. To keep their captive running in Hungary, they will need to pay square footage costs for the floorspace, IT costs, employee recruitment and hiring costs, insurance costs, taxes on the premises, and the list goes on. . .

Example 3: Development for a Huge, Global Manufacturing Company

Even the largest and richest of companies sometimes struggle with expanding their teams quickly and cost-effectively. A multi-billion pound (dollar) global manufacturing company has engaged a team of AoteA developers using our standard IT offshoring model, which provides a dedicated team in a dedicated branch office environment that's fully integrated into the customer's environment and culture.

The company granted their offshore team access to a lengthy backlog of projects and maintenance work, and steers them at every sprint to work on the most urgent needs. This company chose AoteA because, unlike traditional outsourcing firms, our model allows them to direct their offshore team to be agile and change tack according to their business needs at each sprint.

Now that the company has contracted with AoteA, they no longer need to consider hiring extra contractors, expanding their IT footprint, or increasing their floor space. They have also stopped engaging in fixed project models with traditional outsourcing firms, which reduced their agility—and levied them with fluctuating monthly costs!

AoteA's approach, and ideally located ODC, make it easy for our customer's product managers and project managers to communicate with the team daily, both verbally and through written media. The team's English is nearly perfect!

This initiative has been so successful that the offshore team is now engaged to write embedded software for the company's key products and core business offerings.

Example 4: Service Desk
This is not simply a cost exercise. Service Desks take up space and require many resources. Yes, they receive lower pay. But, the 24/7 shift patterns and the sheer number of desks mean they are often highly expensive to collocate with your customers. Offshoring a Service Desk results in a substantial cost reduction. However, as with all things "service-related," communication is key.

In recent years, several UK banks have brought their Service Desks back from India. As office space in London costs a fortune, they located them in lower-cost areas of the UK, such as South Wales, Scotland, and North East England. This shift resulted in a huge improvement in the standard of support, but at a significant cost. What if you could have the best of both worlds?

East Africa is an ideal location for offshoring a Service Desk, as both the standard of English and the technical knowledge of the staff are exceptional. East Africans often have accents that sound more British than those you might find on the Indian subcontinent, or in the Philippines. It's particularly important for Service Desk workers to be easily understood by callers from the Western World. The more familiar the accent, the more relaxed the customer, and the easier it is to handle the call.

The average salary for a Service Desk worker in South Wales is approximately £16000 per annum. Add in employer's taxes and office costs, and this employee ends up costing you over £2000 (approximately USD 2500) per month.

Now consider this: *By offshoring your Service Desk to AoteA's ODC in East Africa, you could save 30% or more on those costs **AND** simultaneously eliminate the costs of hiring, taxation, health care, vacations, and more!*

Example 5: 24/7 Service Desk for a Global Medical Customer

A global medical company with offices in New Zealand, Australia, Europe, Britain, and America engaged AoteA to set up and manage, for one year, a 24/7 Service Desk. This was part of a corporate review and transition initiative aimed at reducing their overall internal IT footprint, with the goal of eventually moving the Service Desk function to fit within their existing call centre staff over time.

By utilising AoteA's expertise, we were able to set them up with proper ITIL processes and measurements and recommend and configure a suitable Service Desk platform. Over the year, we handled their internal facing services incidents and requests, hugely reducing their monthly costs— not just in terms of salaries, but also floor space. (They reduced the area they had occupied by half and rented the other half to another company.)

As we refined their processes and Service Desk configuration to fit their business better, we also ramped up their non-IT-focused, external facing, customer service call centre to handle incoming IT-focused calls. After the year was up, their software, processes and people were all fully briefed and equipped to handle these calls. Previously. an entirely separate Service Desk was required to perform these tasks.

Example 6: Network Operations Centre (NOC)

A huge, global non-governmental organisation (NGO) was working with one of our partner companies to see if they could eradicate fraud in their education programme. This NGO works with governments of Third World countries to expand their education programmes, especially in rural and deprived areas. The problem was that local officials were taking the money for the schooling of the kids and falsifying the attendance records. The NGO was losing hundreds of millions of dollars every year to this fraud.

The partner company has a system that checks children into school in the morning and tracks them throughout the day. Their movements can then be checked against known fraud patterns. The system issues an alert in real time when suspicious activity is detected, so observers can be dispatched to confirm the fraud.

AoteA was able to provide a solution for monitoring hundreds of locations worldwide with a small team based in East Africa. The cost of this monitoring was negligible compared to the amount of money the NGO saved by avoiding these fraudulent schools.

This same system, modified, can be used to monitor environmental parameters in residential or industrial buildings, allowing timely intervention by safety or security services, and protecting lives and equipment. The system, which was developed in tandem with AoteA, makes monitoring simple to set up and is very cost effective.

Chapter 12   A Cost-effective Solution

So, now that you've reached the end of this book, you know how IT offshoring eliminates the negatives associated with traditional IT outsourcing. It's time to kick old-school outsourcing firms to the curb and embrace AoteA's offshoring model, which offers a plenitude of benefits, such as these:

- Dramatic reduction in costs
- No degradation in security
- Stable, flexible, effective branch office
- Fewer time zone or language barriers between the home and branch office
- Ability to "ramp up" without the high costs of hiring onshore workers
- Ability to "ramp down," if required, without the pain and expense of layoffs in the home office
- Increased retention of in-house IT staff
- Decreased costs of maintaining legacy systems
- Dramatically lower risk of failure

Many Fortune 1000 companies have already put their own effective IT offshoring strategies into practice by building global captive centres. This approach is easier for them to implement, because they have the resources to establish networks and credibility in countries and regions suitable for IT offshoring. But what about the other 90% of businesses and non-profits that don't have the luxury of resources to build their own captive centres? Are they doomed to work with ineffective IT outsourcing companies forever? Or, should they give up on outsourcing altogether and be confined to expensive local labour rates?

Fortunately, there is a cost-effective solution: You can quickly and easily plug into the experience and expertise of AoteA. We are a pioneer in IT offshoring and have invested years in developing the systems, infrastructure, network, and reputation necessary to provide top quality, state-of-the-art offshoring development centres in East Africa.

AoteA aims mostly to supplement your teams, not completely replace them. We like to help enable organisations of all sizes—even charities and start-ups—that would be unlikely to progress without the costs savings offshoring affords. Regardless of your company's size, we can help you grow and bring your products to market more quickly.

Once we learn your requirements, we go to work putting together a solution tailored to you. The typical response upon reading our proposal is "Is that all?" regarding price.

So, the choice is yours: You can try to develop your own IT offshoring arrangement. Or, you can talk with AoteA to explore your options. Why not give us a call and let us set up a solution tailored to your needs? If you're in the U.S., you'll be speaking directly with me, one of the owners and the head of our U.S. presence. Readers outside the U.S. can visit our website (www.aotea.global) to find the appropriate contact for their area.

Regardless of whether you choose to partner with us or open your own offshore facility, I want to thank you for reading this book. Feel free to share it with someone you know who might be interested in IT offshoring.

Frank Howard

Partner and VP, U.S.

AoteA Global Services, Ltd.

3470 Olney-Laytonsville Road, #296

Olney, MD 20832

Cell: 301-704-2015 | Office: 240-389-0867

Frank.Howard@aotea.global | www.aotea.global

info@LarchmontPublishing.com

102

Bibliography

Gulati, Richa and Carrera, Lucia. "An Evidence-based Approach to Global Talent-Sourcing: Insights from the Oil & Gas Industry." Towers Watson, 2012. https://www.towerswatson.com/en/Insights/IC-Types/Ad-hoc-Point-of-View/2012/An-Evidence-based-Approach-to-Global-Talent-Sourcing-Insights-from-the-Oil--Gas-Industry. (accessed November 22, 2017)

Rob Handfield, SCRC. "A Brief History of Outsourcing." *SCM website*: North Carolina State University, Poole College of Management. https://scm.ncsu.edu/scm-articles/article/a-brief-history-of-outsourcing. (accessed October 15, 2017)

Knapp, Donna. *A Guide to Service Concepts*, 4th Ed. Boston, MA: Course Technology (Cengage Learning), 2014. 13-19.

Santanam, Raghu. Cyber Security, Cyber Crime and Cyber Forensics: Applications and Perspectives (Advances in Digital Crime, Forensics, and Cyber Terrorism), 1st Ed. IGI Global, 2010.

About the Author

Frank Howard is Vice President of AoteA Global Services Ltd. and heads up the company's United States division. AoteA is an innovator in the IT offshoring industry and a leading provider of IT offshoring services with operations based in East Africa and sales offices in several countries around the globe. As one of the company's key partners, Frank adds 30 years of IT-related business acumen and creative solution-building expertise to his colleagues' decades of IT outsourcing/offshoring experience. His primary role at AoteA is to help clients maximise the ROI on their IT resources.

Throughout his career, Frank has established himself as a thought leader, an "idea guy" who thinks outside the box, and a proven builder of long-term relationships with clients.

Frank served in the U.S. Air Force and attended Old Dominion University, where he earned his Bachelor of Science in Electrical Engineering. He is active in his community as a volunteer and has served as a member of the Board of Directors for local non-profit organisations.

www.ingramcontent.com/pod-product-compliance
Lightning Source LLC
Chambersburg PA
CBHW061607220326
41598CB00024BC/3478